THE CITY WITHIN THE HEART

The City Within the Heart

R. C. ZAEHNER

CROSSROAD · NEW YORK

1981
The Crossroad Publishing Company
575 Lexington Avenue, New York, NY 10022

Printed in the United States of America

Library of Congress Catalog Card Number: 81-67830
ISBN: 0-8245-0109-8

Acknowledgements

The heirs of the late R. C. Zaehner and the Publishers wish to thank Professor Lee Siegel, Assistant Professor of Religion, University of Hawaii, who originally discussed this collection with Professor Zaehner, and without whose devoted work this book would never have come into being.

They also wish to thank the following for permission to reprint previously published essays: The Friends of Dr Williams's Library for *Which God is Dead?* first given as a lecture at Dr Williams's Library 1974; *Mysticism Without Love* first published by Cambridge University Press in the journal Religious Studies; *The Wickedness of Evil*, Encounter, Vol. XLII, No 4, April 1974; *Why Not Islam?* first published by Cambridge University Press in the journal Religious Studies.

After exhaustive enquiries, it appears that *Tantum religio potuit suadere malorum*, *The Scandal of Christ*, *The God of the Philosopher*, and *The Holy and Undivided Trinity* have not previously been published. If by any chance any of these pieces have been previously published, the heirs of the late Professor R. C. Zaehner would be glad to be informed so that appropriate acknowledgement may be made in a later impression of this volume.

Contents

Introduction

R. C. Zaehner was a scholar, and this is the book of a scholar: but it is not a work of scholarship; it uses scholarship, rather than contributing to it. The reader can easily see the evidence of Zaehner's deep learning in Oriental religions, but the book is not primarily addressed to the learned. It is addressed, rather, to anybody interested in religion, and discusses problems which need to be resolved by anyone who, in our time of confusion and uncertainty, wants to attain some clarity about religious questions. In this, it is like many of his later books. Zaehner was a scholar who turned into something different, something of more importance than a scholar. Absurdly, there is no reasonable word in English for what he became, I suppose because the thing itself is rare and little respected. In one place I wrote of him after his death that he was a scholar who turned into a sage; and, remembering his appearance, his stature just more than diminutive, his round face and his round pebble glasses, I find the word 'sage' tempting. But it is not right: a sage is a solemn person, and Zaehner, though the most serious, was the least solemn of men. Besides, the word is a misdescription of what he did and aimed to do. A sage purports to know the answers, and enunciates them, lucidly or cryptically according to temperament. But Zaehner's gift, and his aim, was not to pronounce judgement, but to question and provoke. His talent lay in seeing what to ask, rather than how to answer: he was himself tormented by the questions he raised, and perpetually dissatisfied with his own answers. On another occasion, I described him as having become a *penseur*; but this word, too, rings false in English ears. We have scholars and scientists; we have professional philosophers; we have popularisers – people who write popular science and popular history; and we have journalists. We hardly allow a place for those who think hard about important questions of general interest that do not fall within the scope of philosophy as it is currently practised. That was what Zaehner devoted most of the later part of his life to doing.

The transformation occurred because of his appointment as Spalding Professor of Eastern Religions and Ethics in the

University of Oxford in succession to the first occupant of the Chair, Sir Sarvepalli Radhakrishnan, who had resigned to become Vice-President, and later President, of India. Zaehner's appointment was a surprising one. He had hitherto been a Persian scholar and expert on Zoroastrianism. If an Eastern religion is one that originated in what we count as the continent of Asia, then practically all religious are Eastern, so presumably that is not the criterion intended by those who devised the title of the Chair. There is a certain evident contrast between Judaism, Christianity and Islam, on the one hand, and Hinduism, Buddhism, Jainism and Taoism on the other, with the Sikh religion virtually alone in the middle ground. If only the members of the latter group are to be counted as Eastern religions, then Zoroastrianism clearly belongs with the former group, and is thus not an Eastern religion in the intended sense. If the subject in which Zaehner was to be a professor is seen in this light, he was appointed knowing very little about it; nevertheless, the appointment proved to have been an inspired one, for what he lacked, at the outset, in knowledge, he made up in aptitude. In his inaugural lecture, he demonstrated both his independence of mind and his concern to ask searching questions. An Oxford inaugural lecture is a very formal affair. The Vice-Chancellor attends, preceded by the mace-bearer, and the new Professor delivers his lecture in full academic dress. The opening of the lecture is almost formalised: the lecturer devotes a paragraph to extolling his predecessor and his great contributions to the subject, and then, making an abrupt change of topic, launches into the lecture proper. Zaehner ignored tradition. Standing at a lectern, his head only just visible above it, in the hall of All Souls College, looking, with his glasses and his academic cap, very like an owl, he delivered a robust attack on certain of the views not only of his predecessor but of the founder of the Chair, giving and mercilessly refuting quotations from their works. Probably it was in bad taste; it certainly was very witty, and it certainly also gave great offence. But it was not Zaehner's aim to give offence: he had very little of the academic's malice, as he had very little of the academic's *amour propre*. What concerned him was to make clear from the start of his tenure of the Chair that he was nobody else's man. He had formed the impression that the Chair had been founded to propagate a kind of universalism: all religions embody the same essential truths, under different guises, all are different paths to the same ultimate goal. He thought it wrong that the holder of any university post should be committed to any particular view of his subject. He thought, also, that universalism of this kind reduces comparative religion to triviality: if what differentiates the various religions from one another is of minor importance, what is the point of studying them? He wanted, therefore, to declare publicly that he did not adhere to this universalism, and would tell the truth about his subject, as he saw it, undistorted by any propagandist aims. He posed the question of what these complexes of beliefs and practices have in common in virtue of which we call each of them a 'religion'. He did not attempt to answer this question; instead, he confessed to finding them so different from one another that he could perceive nothing whatever in common between them, and was, accordingly, perplexed about whether the expression 'a religion' had any clear sense at all.

It is evident that Zaehner later abandoned this extreme position. He always had too much respect for the particular character of each of the religions that he studied to agree that they were all the same *au fond*; he paid them the compliment of treating the peculiarities of their beliefs and practices as having the importance that they claimed for them. But he was no longer impelled to take up a stance so diametrically opposed to universalism as that adopted in his inaugural lecture. That he was capable of perceiving affinities as well as differences can be seen in the last chapter of this book, in which he attempts to render the Christian doctrine of the Trinity intelligible by appeal to the Vedānta and to Aristotle.

His inaugural lecture delivered, Zaehner settled down to make himself master of his subject. He had a prodigious gift for languages, and would sometimes learn a new one for fun: he could read Sanskrit, Pāli and Arabic as well as Pahlavi, and proceeded to wade through the Hindu and Buddhist scriptures, the writings of the Sūfīs and the two great Indian epics. There followed a stupendous volume of publications: during his tenure of the Chair, he averaged nearly a book a year. He had a great facility for writing, and an enormous appetite for work. Although he had a talent for friendship, a deep affection for a number of particular close friends and an appreciation of human personality, especially for anything bizarre or eccentric, he was not at all dependent upon company and passed a great deal of his time alone, most of it in his study working: he particularly relished the month of August, when All Souls College, a Fellowship at which was attached to the Chair, was closed, and he could pursue his work undisturbed, cooking rudimentary meals for himself in one of the small pantries. Some of his books, like *Zurvān* and *Hindu and Muslim Mysticism*, were works of scholarship; others, like *Hinduism*, were brilliant examples of popular exposition. But he gave himself more and more to the production of books like the present one, books in which he *used* his profound knowledge of the great religions to inquire into urgent questions about religion in general.

What first impelled him in this direction was his preoccupation with the nature of mysticism. 'Indian religious thinking', he wrote, 'is mystical through and through'; and so, if he were to understand Indian religion, he must understand mysticism. Now mysticism is very dear to that universalism which Zaehner had begun his career as professor by denouncing: it has been reiterated again and again that 'mysticism is essentially one and the same', that all mystical experience is alike an apprehension of the one ultimate reality, that, in it, all religions converge, the doctrinal trappings fall away and the pure essence of religion appears unadorned. But Zaehner, examining the varieties of mystical experience, did not find it so. Certainly the mystics' *interpretations* of their experiences were very various; but Zaehner held not merely that mystical experience is liable to misinterpretation but that, in different forms of mysticism, the experiences themselves differed radically in character. This is not at all to say that the distinct types of mysticism can be classified simply according to the religion within which they are manifested: on the contrary, within the same religious tradition different types of mysticism can occur. Zaehner was not concerned only to characterise the differing interpretations put upon mystical experience, or even the varieties of that experience itself: he was even more deeply concerned to discover what actually happened in mystical states, what each type of mystical experience was an experience *of*. His continuing anxiety to arrive at a satisfactory answer to this question is apparent, as in so much of his writing, in this, his last book.

In addition to the old claim about the essential unity of all mystical experience, Zaehner had also to consider another claim, foreshadowed by William James, anticipated by Aldous Huxley, and now advanced by the exponents of the youth culture: that, while mystical experience indeed affords an otherwise inaccessible insight into the nature of reality, it can be attained at less cost than by ascetic practices, religious exercises or a virtuous life, namely by means of hallucinogenic chemicals. Though an examination of this claim is not strictly the task of a professor of comparative religion, Zaehner, concerned as he was to know the truth about mysticism, felt bound to assess it; and so he inquired into it, himself experimenting with mescaline in the process. This was the start of his interest in the youth culture, with its substitutes for religion and its search for fresh sources of religion. He had great sympathy with it: he understood very well the impatience with established religion, the disgust with the complacency and crassness of a culture dominated by science, the attraction towards Indian religion and Zen Buddhism. His outstanding talent was, in fact, his ability to understand, as from within, any of a most heterogeneous range of ideas and attitudes; he never wrote about anything until he had attained such an understanding of it. He was never content merely to enunciate dispassionately any given set of ideas: he wished to convey what it was like to accept them, how the world appeared to one who took them to be true. The present book, indeed, contains a number of virtuoso exercises of this talent. It was because he had this gift that he was able, in his writings, to communicate so directly with all those who are perplexed about fundamental religious questions.

The attitude for which Zaehner felt least sympathy was, I think, that which has become predominant in our society, that of the man who has become wholly unresponsive to all religious feelings and ideas. Even of this attitude he essays a sympathetic account in Chapter 4 of this book, in terms not of an irreligious modern man, but of his classical counterpart, Lucretius. But, although this chapter ends with the words 'Perhaps we are better off without it', that is, without religion, the book does not go on to *argue* that we cannot, after all, do without it: it is not really addressed, any more than Zaehner's other books were, to someone who does not see the point of bothering with religion. The chapter is intended to provoke the religious reader, not to pose the question whether we have need of religion at all; although he was tormented by many problems about religion, I do not think that Zaehner was capable of taking *that* question very seriously, if for no other reason than that the reality of mystical experience was too evident to him for the question to be a live one.

Zaehner never confused understanding with agreement; and, though he was sympathetic with the youth culture, he was particularly fascinated by one manifestation of it on whom all but the most perverse judgements would be severe – Charlie Manson, who is discussed again in the present book. Before a visit to the United States, he wrote to the university that had invited him announcing that he would lecture on Aristotle and Charlie Manson. Since neither subject can have been what they were expecting from a professor of Eastern religions, they replied that they would prefer something on Hinduism, but he answered that it would have to be Aristotle and Charlie Manson or nothing. This was partly due to the obsessive quality of his intellectual processes: he could never pursue more than one sustained train of thought at a time; during a period when he was engaged on some topic, all his thought, and most of his conversation, were devoted to it. But his fascination with Charlie Manson was not, or very little, due to a taste for the macabre. It was because he understood, and took seriously, the ideas underlying Manson's conduct; he thought it important to discover how far that conduct really was the logical outcome of those ideas. In the same way, he concerned himself with much else that does not ordinarily fall within the scope of comparative religion: not only with Aristotle, whose ideas about God are discussed in this volume, but also, for a time, with Marxism, which he regarded (mistakenly, I am inclined to think) as having the characteristics of a religion. He paid little attention to contemporary theology, but at one stage conceived a great admiration for Teilhard de Chardin, an admiration which is recanted in this book.

Zaehner was a Catholic convert, and his religion was of deep importance to him; but he did not choose to write to convince others of the truth of his own faith. He wrote, rather, to provide a solid foundation for thought about religion from whatever starting-point; as I said earlier, his concern was rather to frame questions than to supply answers. He was one of those very few

Christians to whom not merely the existence but the appeal of other religions was very vivid. He neither derided them for diverging from Christianity nor patronisingly commended them for approximating to it; in many respects in which he saw quite clearly that they differed from Christianity, he also felt their attraction. In a passage from which Zaehner drew the title of one of his books, the Epistle to the Hebrews opens with the observation that God 'at sundry times and in divers manners spake unto our fathers by the prophets'. Zaehner took very seriously the idea that God has spoken to us not only through the prophets and teachers recorded in the Judaeo-Christian Bible, but 'in divers manners' by other messengers. He therefore felt an urgent need to raise questions of identity; beginning with the question 'What are mystical experiences experiences of?', he wanted to have a means of recognising religious truth, in however unfamiliar a guise, as well as of identifying religious falsehoods, however seductive. Christians in the past have devoted much thought to one question of identity, 'Who are the Jews?'; some even among the saints and fathers of the Church returned answers so lacking in charity as to lead Pope John XXIII to say, 'We have the mark of Cain upon us'. In this book, Zaehner raises many questions of identity, and, in particular, the questions 'Who was Muhammad?' and 'What is Islam?', most Christian answers to which, in the past, have been foolish and ignorant. He does not even claim to have found a satisfactory answer, but I do not think a non-Muslim reader can finish this book without his understanding of Islam deepened. The West has thoughtlessly inherited from its medieval past an attitude to Islamic civilisation as something alien and 'Oriental', when a moment's thought should show that its history is inextricably bound up with our own: co-heirs with us of Greek science and philosophy, of Roman architecture and of Jewish religious tradition, Muslim culture has always had a far greater affinity with that of Europe than with the indigenous cultures of India and the Far East, as well as transmitting far more of value to Europe than Europe ever transmitted to it. It is senseless to treat of the history of Christendom as a unit: the history of Christians, Jews and Muslims can only be dealt with as a whole. For the most part, however, our historians have made no serious attempt to correct this distorted vision, inherited from an age when Muslims, as virtually the only unbelievers known, were often ludicrously credited with being polytheists, and reinforced by European arrogance during the age of imperialism. Indeed, a strong case can be made that, from a cultural standpoint, the history of Persia in pre-Islamic times ought also to be included in the history of 'the West', whereas, in ancient history as traditionally presented, Persia appears only as an external force that from time to time irrupts into the region of classical civilisation, in the same way that Islam does in later history. Zaehner remarks in passing on the debt which the religions of the Judaeo-Christian family owe to Zoroastrianism; by contrast, he brings out clearly how (except for caste) the characteristic features of Indian religion, and therefore of Indian culture, were due not to the Aryan invaders but to the indigenous civilisation which they overran. Reflections of this kind go beyond anything Zaehner is here concerned with; what preoccupied him were more important questions of the truth about religion. But if, in order to understand a culture, it is necessary first to understand its religion, a better start could not be made than by reading Zaehner's writings.

The most fundamental identity question is 'Which God should we believe in and worship?'; and, in the last few years of his life, Zaehner had become troubled by this question. The reader will encounter several different Gods in this book: above all, the God of the prophets and the God of the philosophers. He will not find it easy to see which Zaehner is urging him to believe in, or in which Zaehner himself believes. This posthumous book and the last one Zaehner published while he was alive, *Our Savage God*, bear witness to a kind of crisis through which he was passing: he felt tormenting uncertainties about the identity of the God to whom, as a Christian, he must submit. I am sure that, had he lived, he would have resolved these uncertainties, to the enlightenment of us all. But God did not leave him to attain this resolution in this life: at the age of sixty-one he fell down dead in the street on his way to Sunday evening Mass.

This book consists of articles, lectures and a sermon which Zaehner himself collected together, and redesignated as chapters, to form a book: I think that he must already have been planning the book when he chose the subjects for the lectures and articles. He had not chosen a title for it, however: the present title was suggested by Mr Lee Siegel, one of his students. It is taken from a translation of the *Chāndogya Upanisad* made by Zaehner himself:

> Never on earth can a man bring back one close to him once he has departed this life so that he can see him. Yet whatever he may long for among the living and the dead, or whatever else he may long for and cannot obtain, all that he will find if he will but go to that city of Brahman within the heart; for there it is that his real desires are, though now they are covered over with unreality.

MICHAEL DUMMETT

[handwritten annotations:]

≠ India
soma
warriors

breath
make
- robe
le
imagining

fulfilled

Remember
what you need to
remember
Forget what you need
to forget

keep them in your
heart
& drive them from
your mind.

Chapter 1

Which God is Dead?

It is now some twenty-two years since I became the Spalding Professor of Eastern Religions and Ethics in the University of Oxford. At the time of my election the subject of comparative religion, the history of religion, *Religionswissenschaft* (call it what you will since I do not propose to waste your time with definitions of this curiously ambivalent thing) was a relatively new discipline (if that is the right word) in this country, at least as the term was understood by H. N. Spalding, the founder of the Chair. Certainly Social Anthropology as it had been developed under the brilliant auspices of that highly individualistic near-genius, the late Sir Evan Evans-Pritchard, was already a flourishing postgraduate school, but Social Anthropology was primarily concerned with the study of existing non-literate societies or 'primitive' cultures as they had once been called. This was certainly not the kind of study H. N. Spalding had in mind when he founded the new Chair. He was not interested, except peripherally, in the religious and magical insights of non-literate tribes, but in the great religions of the world as they have come down to us in history in all their bewildering ramifications, their glaring discords and in what he thought might be their underlying harmony.

'The purpose of the Professorship', he wrote in his preamble to the statute inaugurating the Chair, 'shall be to build up in the University of Oxford a permanent interest in the great religious and ethical systems . . . of the East, . . . to set forth their development and spiritual meaning, and to interpret them by comparison and contrast with each other and with the religions and ethics of the West . . . , with the aim of bringing together the world's great religions in closer understanding, harmony, and friendship'.

I am painfully conscious of the fact that I have totally failed to achieve any (or almost any) of the objectives Mr Spalding had in mind. At the same time I cannot blame myself for this since, by upbringing, I am an academic, and the typical academic virtues are objectivity so far as that is possible, attention to detail, and an unprejudiced assessment of the evidence: in a word pedantry. What Mr Spalding was asking for, however, was not pedantry but creative imagination. So far as I have tried to do anything consciously it has been to enliven academic pedantry with a little sympathetic insight into religions other than my own.

Today the situation has greatly changed. Traditional theology as taught in the older universities continues to decline whereas 'comparative religion' or 'religious studies' as it has now come to be called thrives and shows every sign of continuing to thrive and to expand since it obviously fulfils a need in our society which is no longer Christian even in name: for do not Christians themselves speak of a post-Christian society as if traditional Christianity were already dead and buried?

This is scarcely surprising because it is the Christians themselves who have been busily digging their own graves to the greater glory of nobody quite knows who. The process can be painful, and an intensive study of the other great religions of mankind can scarcely fail to make the process even more painful; for, to go no further than our own Semitic tradition, it is quite clear that traditional Christianity's claim to possess the whole truth is matched by an equally consistent claim put forward by the older dispensation of the Jews and the newer one of Islam. Israel is simply not interested in what she considers to be the extraordinary perversions of her strictly monotheistic religion by Edom (with whom she identifies Christianity) or with the new dispensation of the house of Ishmael as proclaimed by the Arabian prophet Muhammad. Similarly the Muslims, because the theophany that came down upon Muhammad in the shape of the Koran, the 'Word made Book', necessarily abrogates both the Torah, the covenant vouchsafed to the Jews through *their* prophet, Moses, and the *Injīl*, the 'Evangelium' or Gospel which Jesus, the son of Mary the Virgin, received as a corrective to the more ancient dispensation. Thus we have the somewhat absurd situation of three monotheistic religions, sprung from the same root, each so certain of its own 'truth' that until quite recently each was quite happy to develop its own theology in total disregard of the other two. It is true that Christianity today has become increasingly interested in its own Jewish roots at the expense of what are now considered to be 'inauthentic' Hellenistic accretions, but, with the sole exceptions of Bishop Kenneth Cragg and Father Sano Bassetti, Christian theology can scarcely be said to have even tried to grapple with the problems raised by what Muslims consider to be the final revelation of the one true God to man in the Koran, God's eternal Word appearing in time not as 'flesh', that is, the man Jesus, but as Book, which to the rational mind would appear to be a very much more sensible proposition.

However, the new discipline of 'religious studies' is supplanting the older one of theology in the newer universities not because many of them offer courses in Jewish studies or Islam but because they concern themselves ever more with the religions of India – Hinduism and Buddhism – and these are religions so radically different from traditional Christianity that some Christians still wonder whether they can be counted as religions at all.

On Monday 23 November 1654 from about 10.30 p.m. until about half past midnight, you may remember, Pascal had a religious experience of overwhelming intensity: the only word which seemed to give any adequate representation of its terrific impact was 'fire'. That this was a *mystical* experience (at least as 'mystical' is interpreted by practically all writers on that elusive subject today) is shown by the lapidary words with which he characterises the nature of this 'fire': 'Certainty. Certainty. Feeling. Joy. Peace. . . . Forgetfulness of the world and of all things except God. . . . Greatness of the human soul. . . . Joy. Joy, Joy, tears of joy. . . . Renunciation, total and sweet.'

Renunciation, joy, peace, and above all certainty: these four characteristics would appear to be common to nearly all forms of religious mysticism. We might go so far as to say that they are writ large in the 'mainline' mystical traditions of both Christianity and Islam on the Semitic side and Hinduism and Buddhism on the Indian. I have, however, left out everything specifically Christian from Pascal's *mémorial*, since any student of mysticism will and must allow for sectarian interpretation of an experience that seems to transcend all the doctrinal differences that separate the various religions and give them their individual stamp. But to go on to argue from this, as is the fashion these days, that because human language is not equipped to deal with states that transcend ordinary experience, these states must necessarily be one and the same seems to me about as sensible as to assert that because a blind man cannot perceive light, therefore, should he have an inner apprehension of light, it must always be the same and that the different colours which everyone gifted with the sense of sight sees are simply 'interpretations' of that one thing, light. The same analogy would hold good for the tone-deaf; for just as the tone-deaf man can distinguish degrees of volume of noise, but not the varieties of pitch, so can the mystic have experiences of greater or less intensity, but these experiences will not be different in kind.

Pascal, however, thought otherwise; and I am naive enough to suppose that a man of his very exceptional intelligence who had had an overwhelming experience of 'God' probably knew what he was talking about rather better even than the best 'objective' writers on mysticism, the most serious-minded of whom would still appear to be William James who reached a superficially similar 'certainty' after he had taken a dose of nitrous oxide, the LSD of his day. What, however, Pascal makes abundantly clear is that the 'God' he had experienced was the 'God of Abraham, God of Isaac, God of Jacob, *not* of the philosophers and scientists'. As a philosopher and scientist in addition to being a Christian he should surely know.

In my generation at least (unless one happened to be what is called a cradle Catholic) one was very soon introduced to the God of Abraham, God of Isaac, and God of Jacob and to 'him whom thou has sent, Jesus Christ'. Most of us children were bored, almost all confused since in those prim old days our teachers were very careful to keep us in ignorance of what fornication and adultery really meant (and the Old Testament cannot make much sense if this essential information is withheld) nor had most of us any idea of what John the Baptist was doing when he leapt in his mother's womb: how could we since we were never told what a womb was? Far worse, however, was that the more thoughtful of us could not help being appalled at the violence, the vindictiveness, and the sheer favouritism of the God we were bidden to worship. The result should have been anticipated by anyone who was still capable of reading the Old Testament with the eyes of a child and not with those of an indoctrinated theologian: when the intelligent child grew up he violently questioned the validity of this sanguinary document and turned away to agnosticism, atheism, Marxism or whatever. There was nowhere else to turn since the Eastern religions had as yet not percolated through to the young. Typical cases of this reaction were, of course, Aldous Huxley and C. G. Jung.

Jung was the son of a Protestant pastor and he had the misfortune to have a naturally mystical temperament which began to show itself at a very early age; or perhaps it would be more accurate to say that he had a pantheistic temperament, as his contemporary Pierre Teilhard de Chardin was often to say of himself. God he could discern in nature all right but not in church. It was, then, scarcely surprising that his first Communion, for which he had been meticulously prepared, proved to be a shattering experience. 'Slowly', he wrote, 'I came to understand that this communion had been a fatal experience for me. It had proved hollow; more than that, it had proved to be a total loss. I knew I would never again be able to participate in this ceremony. "Why, that is not religion at all", I thought. "It is an absence of God; the church is a place I should not go to. It is not life which is there, but death". '[1]

From that moment, for Jung, God *was* dead. But which God? Precisely the 'God of Abraham, God of Isaac, God of Jacob' who had ravished Pascal's soul. Why should this have been? Pascal's experience, so far from turning him away from Christianity, had given it a new and undreamed of dimension. Jung's experience of the God he described in nature made him reject his father's Christianity as a hollow sham. In other words Jung had never experienced the God of his father since it had never occurred to his father that God is someone or something that can be experienced: Pascal experienced him as a blazing fire and his experience confirmed him in his belief in an intensely living God, at once terrible and kind, the God of the Old Testament quite as much as of the New. What Jung had experienced, on the other hand, was the God of the philosophers, the God of Spinoza, who is simply another word for Nature. This God he knew to be alive, and this is the God he was later to discover when he began to interest himself in Indian and Chinese religion. This is the hidden God for whom so many young people who have found nothing of value in Christianity are now looking. He is

Mystic

not the God of faith, since faith is as characteristic of Islam as it is of Christianity (and the two 'faiths' are confessedly at loggerheads with each other); rather it is a God who, given the right dispositions, can be experienced here and now: or so we are told.

Plainly, if religion is to have any meaning at all, there must be an element of experience in it: there must be some apperception of what, for lack of a more precise word, we must still call the divine, the holy, or, if you prefer Rudolf Otto's word, the numinous. One marked tendency in most of the Christian churches today is to attempt to eliminate this 'numinous' element altogether and to reduce religion to purely human terms, which would seem to amount to voiding the Christ of orthodoxy of his divinity and to reduce him to his allegedly perfect humanity. In an increasingly secular age we are asked to be sensible, to face the fact that the Christ of the creeds *is* dead and that, if we are honest with ourselves, we will have to admit that this is so. Hence few of us still speak in terms of God becoming man so that man may, in a sense, become God, but would prefer to take Jesus as the model which we should seek to follow. The function of the Church would, then, no longer appear to be to sanctify the world but rather to accept the world as it is and enter into it without any view to sanctifying or 'divinising' it. In other words the Church must accept secularisation with a good grace: it must desacralise, that is desecrate itself, thereby abolishing all distinction between the carnal and the divine.

There is much to be said for this approach, and it has been cogently argued by my friend Professor J. G. Davies in his recent book *Every Day God.*[2] And yet, and yet . . . Something is missing, and this something is precisely that element of the 'numinous' which is the subject of the relentless criticism of Professor Davies's fair but uncompromising book.

Professor Davies is nothing if not honest. Much of his earlier work was devoted to 'mysticism' and, like so many others, he fell under the spell of William Blake, but then he began to question not the validity but the relevance of the whole grand edifice. It was no doubt highly relevant in the great ages of faith, but did it mean anything much to anyone today? His answer in *Every Day God* is a slightly qualified rather than an absolute No. Let the numinous have their numinosity if they must, but let them not claim that this is of the essence of Christianity which has nothing to do with Otto's 'wholly Other' beyond the heavens but everything to do with the *man Jesus who by bringing the 'numinous' into the bustle* and worry of the Palestine of his day thereby abolished all distinction between the numinous and the ordinary, the sacred and the profane.

That this is not only a possible but also a fruitful transvaluation of traditional Christian values would seem to be proved by the flourishing state of theological studies in the University of Birmingham over which Professor Davies presides: the kids like it, as the Americans would say. But not all of them.

There still remains a minority, sometimes a very vocal one which feels that life must ultimately lack meaning unless it has a transcendental dimension, which means, I suppose, unless it is in some way anchored in eternity. More often than one thinks, perhaps, young people do have such 'intimations of immortality' which, though they may be vague enough, nevertheless make them think that behind the physical world there lies another world which is more real than this world of space and time simply because they sense, again however vaguely, that this other world can and does make itself felt on rare occasions, usually in moments of solitude and in natural surroundings of exceptional beauty – mountains, the sea, the blossoming of spring, and, of course, sunsets. They may or may not associate such blessed intimations with a God indwelling Nature or they may interpret them on purely aesthetic lines, but that they strike them as some kind of revelation can scarcely be in doubt.

That these 'revelations' are not nearly so rare as is sometimes supposed is the message of a recent book appropriately entitled *Inglorious Wordsworths* by Michael Paffard of Keele University who sent a questionnaire to teenage schoolchildren and undergraduates asking them to describe any 'Wordsworthian' experiences they might have had. Of the 400 young people to whom the questionnaire was sent 222 returned positive answers. This is not perhaps in itself surprising, for the passage which Mr Paffard selected as the touchstone for his 'inglorious Wordsworths' was taken from W. H. Hudson's *Far Away and Long Ago* which, while being clearly 'numinous', could scarcely be called 'mystical' (a word which Mr Paffard rightly avoids). The passage runs as follows:

It was not, I think, until my eighth year that I began to be distinctly conscious of something more than this mere childish delight in nature. It may have been there all the time from infancy – I don't know; but when I began to know it consciously it was as if some hand had surreptitiously dropped something into the honeyed cup which gave it at times a new flavour. It gave me little thrills, at times purely pleasurable, at other times startling, and there were occasions when it became so poignant as to frighten me. The sight of a magnificent sunset was sometimes more than I could endure and made me wish to hide myself away. The feeling, however, was evoked more powerfully by trees than by any other sight; it varied in power according to the time and place and the appearance of the tree or trees, and always affected me most on moonlight nights. Frequently after I had first begun to experience it consciously, I would go out of my way to meet it, and I used to steal out of the house alone when the moon was at its full to stand, silent and motionless, near some group of large trees, gazing at the dusky green foliage silvered by the beams; and at such times the sense of mystery would grow until a sensation of delight would change to fear, and the fear increase until it was no longer to be borne, and I would hastily escape to recover the sense of reality and safety indoors, where there was light and company.

The passage is anodyne enough, but it certainly typifies what Rudolf Otto described as the numinous: something beautiful and fascinating yet at the same time frightening and uncanny. This is not yet mysticism, but rather an intimation of what a mystical state might be like – an intimation, if you like, of that God who pervades all natural things, who was so conspicuously absent from the church where Jung experienced that shattering non-event of his first Communion.

What Mr Paffard's respondents had experienced and what so many of them, like Jung, could not experience in church was precisely a 'communion' with some power that was beyond sense and discursive thought, and this 'God', once experienced in however rudimentary a form, is not dead. The uninhibited advance of technology may well succeed in killing him too, but that is another question too broad to be broached in this context.

For the moment this God is still very much alive and seems to exercise a subtle fascination on many of the young. He is the God of Eastern mysticism, not Pascal's Hebraic God whom he claimed to have experienced in ecstasy, but the ground of the universe which is at the same time the inmost essence of the human soul. To experience *this* God is not just to have an intimation of immortality but to experience immortality itself: it is not just the promise of eternal life accepted on faith in the resurrection of one man but the experience of an eternal form of existence which is beyond both life and death as normally understood and in which 'all at once, as it were out of the intensity of the consciousness of individuality, individuality itself seemed to dissolve and fade away into boundless being, and this not a confused state but the clearest, the surest of the surest, utterly beyond words – where death was an almost laughable impossibility – the loss of personality (if so it were) seeming no extinction, but the only true life,' as Tennyson once wrote to a friend.[3]

The essence of the experience as described by Tennyson is twofold: (i) individuality seems to disappear and is swallowed up into 'boundless being', and consequently (ii) since boundless being is the life of all things, personal death thereby becomes 'an almost laughable impossibility' since the life of the individual is now experienced as the life of the All. *This* God, then, if God is the right name for him or it, cannot die by definition since it is imperishable Being; and this is the 'God of the philosophers' who is both the God of the Hindus as he appears throughout the Upanishads and the God whom Aristotle discovered by dint or arduous, unremitting thought. He is both the Unmoved Mover and the Thinking of Thought (or perhaps 'Consciousness of consciousness' might be a better translation) whose joy consists in the eternal contemplation of himself. And so, says Aristotle:

... it is contemplation that is supremely joyous and supremely good. If, then, it is thus that God possesses the good in eternity, even as we can so do on occasion, it is wonderful indeed: if ever more so, then it is yet more marvellous. But this is just how it is. And [in him] there is life too; for the actuality, activity and energy of Him who is aware (*Nous*) is life, and He is himself that energy and actuality. . . . And so we roundly affirm that God is a living being, eternal and supremely good, and that in God there is life and coherent, eternal being. For that *is* God.[4]

This may well be true, but what is true of the God of Israel is equally true of the God of the philosophers: if he is no longer a living experience, then he might just as well not exist. But Aristotle's claim is that he *can* be experienced ('if, then it is thus that God possesses the good in eternity, *even as we can so do on occasion* . . .'), and that we can really do so is the purport of almost all the Hindu scriptures. But until recently no one pretended that it was easy.

For Aristotle complete blessedness must mean complete independence, but it did not occur to him that such a condition could be permanently enjoyed in this life, for no one can be eternally independent, autarkic, and free except God himself. In the Hebraic legend too our first parents are tempted to eat of the forbidden tree because they are assured by the wise serpent that by so doing they will be 'like gods, knowing good and evil'. In both cases it is assumed that man, being composed of body as well as soul, can never really become like God so long as he remains man. In this the Jews and Aristotle agreed. To be a man means not to be simply a discarnate spirit but to possess a body of some sort, even if this is a 'spiritual body' as St Paul has it or a 'subtle body' as the Hindus would say. This, however, is at variance with practically the whole mystical tradition of both the East and the West which sees the body and matter in general as the prison-house of the soul. Salvation for the Hindu and even more for the Buddhist means freedom from matter and all that conditions matter, freedom from time and space and indeed from individuality itself which it is not easy to conceive of without some material substrate.

Even Christians today are embarrassed by the doctrine of the resurrection of the body: to the Hindus and Buddhists the very idea of it seems not ridiculous but horrific – and real. For both religions are to a certain extent conditioned by their belief in the transmigration of souls: and this, though it may *seem* good to the simple-minded since any accumulation of merit in this life will lead to a more comfortable incarnation next time, is nonetheless the root of all imperfection and in that sense evil. Human life is by definition conditioned: man *qua* man can never be free. Being bound by space and time, by causation and the inexorable laws of *Karma* (the law of automatic reward and punishment for whatever one does), he is ineluctably bound to the wheel of existence since even his good actions cannot bring him freedom but only bind him to the higher states of becoming in the phenomenal world. You may indeed become a god and taste the joys of any one of the heavens, but in the end your store of merit will run out and back you will come to this earth, only to start all over again. Hence, for a Hindu or Buddhist, the resurrection of the body, so far from being an eschatological promise, is an inevitable and dreadful fact, to have done with which means final release from this valley of tears in which we drag out our miserable days – final release which means autarky, independence, and eternal being. For the Buddhists this state can be achieved; for it is the state of 'Enlightenment' or 'Awakening' that the Buddha himself achieved. And, having achieved it, he was able to devise a practical way by following which others could achieve it. However, what he is talking about is not God (for gods like all other sentient beings are subject to birth and death, rebirth and redeath) but a state of being unconditioned by space and time and therefore immortal. 'I do not speak of coming and going, of standing still or falling down, nor of coming to be. [What I speak of] has no base, does not develop, depends on nothing.' For, as he goes on to say, 'something which is neither born nor becomes, which is neither made nor compounded *does* exist'. And because this is so (for the Buddha's enlightenment brought him the unmediated experience of this transcendent state), the way of release can be found.[5]

What the Buddha is describing is, of course, what is usually called Nirvana, the 'eternal rest' that Christians normally associate with death. In a sense indeed it *is* death – but death without rebirth; and that means the end of suffering. For our world has three characteristics: it is impermanent, devoid of substance or self, and *therefore* must be painful, beset with anguish and unease.

That the world should be described in these terms is scarcely surprising particularly in a country with India's detestable climate. The world itself is not evil as it was for the Gnostics and Manichees, but simply unendurably painful, beset with worry, and unease. What is perhaps surprising is that a doctrine which is so pessimistic about the world should appeal to so many of the young today. But is it really surprising? The myth of progress on which we have lived for so long has now been shattered by two world wars which have revealed to us not only the beastliness of man (which is nothing new) but also his immense capacity for diabolic evil which has nothing whatever to do with our animal nature. Further, progress itself has trapped us in a mechanical mass civilisation in which we feel ever more acutely that the Buddha was right: life *is* one long round of unease, anxiety, and pain. Hence the longing of so many young people to escape from it all. Add to this the collapse of Christian values and the demise in ridicule of the traditional Judaeo-Christian God, and the desire of so many to find a way of escape from it all into a 'deathless' state immune from suffering seems very understandable indeed.

William James divided religious man into two categories – the 'healthy-minded' and the 'sick soul'. In our present technological civilisation both classes search for means of escape. The healthy-minded – by which James understood Aristotelian man who accepts his body-soul humanity as given and physical and mental life as a good – these too can now find nothing healthy or good or desirable in our urban anthills: hence they drift off and found communes in the country where they hope to live a life more in accordance with nature. The sick soul – the Platonist and the Gnostic whom we have always had with us and who longs to be rid of the body and all its tawdry trappings – he too now finds yet profounder reasons for his discontent: the modern world is not just painful and riddled with anxiety, it is becoming downright diabolic. Hence the desire of both classes to escape.

James's 'healthy-minded' type is rarely interested in mysticism of any kind. He may, it is true, have had 'Wordsworthian' experiences of the type that Mr Paffard has collected and analysed, or he may even have had the fuller pantheistic or rather 'pan-en-henic' experience in which he has experienced all things as One and One as all. Should he have such an experience he will almost certainly have become convinced that what he has experienced and *seen* is the ultimate truth. It is no longer a question of opinion: he *knows*. This 'knowledge' will almost certainly turn him against any form of organised religion, and should he stumble across the Upanishads (as nowadays he almost certainly will) he will find his intuition amply confirmed; for here are treatises which deliberately turn their back on their own ritualist past and denounce their time-hallowed rituals as 'unstable barks'. As to its practitioners,

> Self-wise, puffed up with learning,
> Passing their days in the midst of ignorance,
> They wander round, the fools, doing themselves much hurt,
> Like blind men guided by the blind.[6]

And what exactly is this 'knowledge' that makes the adept so scornful of his ancestral religion? It is the knowledge, not as in Buddhism that there *is* a way of escape from this world of space and time, but that there is no need to escape at all because your own deepest self is not only *always* free from all conditioning factors (though you do not know it) but also that it is *identical* with the unmoving, eternal ground of the whole cosmos: in other words your essential 'You' *is* the Godhead beyond God. And that is an intoxicating thought. As one of the earliest texts puts it:

This whole universe is Brahman. . . .

He who consists of mind, whose body is the breath of life, whose form is light, whose idea is the real, whose self is space, through whom are all works, all desires, all scents, all tastes, who encompasses all this universe, who does not speak and has no care – he is my Self within the heart, smaller than a grain of rice or a barley-corn, or a mustard-seed, or a grain of millet, or the kernel of a grain of millet; this is my Self within my heart, greater than the earth, greater than the atmosphere, greater than all these worlds.

All works, all desires, all scents, all tastes belong to it: it encompasses all this universe, does not speak and has no care. This my Self within the heart is that Brahman. When I depart from hence I shall merge into it. He who believes this will never doubt.[7]

Or even more plainly: 'This finest essence – the whole universe has it as its Self. That is the Real: That is the Self: That *you* are.[8] The 'finest essence' in question is primal Being, 'One without a second', and that is what you really are.

If this is really true, then not only are you God but you reach out far beyond God into the heart of the Godhead itself, the eternal Now, as Meister Eckhart put it, which is the real You.

The philosophic aspects of this pure monism I have discussed elsewhere. All I would like to do here is to say a word or two about its psychological aspects. 'Healthy-minded' Aristotelian man is not in the least interested in realising himself as God or the Godhead since he is content to be what he is – man. But the 'sick soul', always frustrated, always anxiety-ridden, longs to escape into an unconditioned form of existence and this, no doubt, Buddhism will do for him; but if, in addition, he can convince himself that the real 'he' is actually the Absolute, how much more satisfying that is! Indeed it is the ultimate satisfaction and bliss than which nothing *can* be higher. But how can you get there?

Already in 1902 William James had discovered that these unitive mystical states could be induced by drugs – in his case nitrous oxide. Pragmatist and empiricist though he was, he felt himself compelled to testify to the authenticity of his experience:

> One conclusion was forced upon my mind at that time, and my impression of its truth has ever since remained unshaken. It is that our normal waking consciousness, rational consciousness as we call it, is but one special type of consciousness, whilst all about it, parted from it by the flimsiest of screens, there lie potential forms of consciousness entirely different. . . . Looking back on my own experiences, they all converge towards a kind of insight to which I cannot help ascribing some metaphysical significance. The keynote is invariably a reconciliation. It is as if the opposites of the world, whose contradictions and conflict make all our difficulties and troubles, were melted into unity.[9]

And this is, of course, perhaps the standard theme of Hindu mystical thinking: the 'All' – the infinitely multiple – melts into the absolutely One which, like Aristotle's God, is 'life and coherent, eternal Being'. This God, so far from being dead, is actually always alive within you and can be actualised and brought to the surface by the application of the appropriate stimulus – by nitrous acid in the case of James, by mescaline in the case of Aldous Huxley, by LSD in countless others.

The debate on drugs and mysticism still goes on in a desultory way, and I have no wish to revive it yet again since it now seems to have moved on to a different level. Drugs, it now seems to be generally admitted, cannot be relied on to release the divine spark – the eternal One within us – but may also lead to a bad trip, what William James called a 'diabolical mysticism'. Hence the disaffected young are turning more and more to Indian gurus and Japanese roshis who claim to lead them 'from the unreal to the real, from darkness to the light, from death to immortality'[10] in the old-fashioned way – without drugs, without sex, without alcohol. And the amazing thing is that there are many who cheerfully make this threefold sacrifice and are often rewarded with a great peace of mind. The price they pay is that they surrender themselves entirely to the guru; and if, as gurus usually claim, they have actually realised their identity with the One, and if the One, as the Hindu texts tell us, is beyond good and evil, there would seem to be dangers even here. But is this not what one would expect? For the God of Abraham, God of Isaac, God of Jacob, himself declares that good and evil proceed from his mouth.[11] What, then, would one expect from the Absolute who, according to *his* scripture, 'does not speak and has no care'?

Chapter 2

Mysticism without Love

'Mysticism means to isolate the eternal from the originated.'[1] This is not my definition of the word 'mysticism' but that of the founder of the 'orthodox' school of Muslim mysticism, Al-Junayd of Baghdad who flourished in the ninth century AD. In actual fact it is not a definition of mysticism at all but of the Arabic word *tawhīd* which means primarily 'the affirmation of unity'; and that surely is an essential ingredient of any form of mysticism: it is the affirmation *through personal experience* of unity either absolutely or in some qualified sense.

oneness

In a Muslim context the word *tawhīd* necessarily means the affirmation of the absolute unity of *God* since this is the first and indispensable dogma of Islam. As for the Hebrews, to be God means to be One – One without a second as the Hindu sacred books put it; or again, 'he does not beget nor is he begotten', as the Koran prefers to say in opposition to what they consider to be the crypto-polytheistic Christian doctrine of the Trinity.

However, what is most significant about Junayd's definition of 'mysticism' is that he makes no mention of love – and this seems surprising since the theme of all his predecessors was that the essence of their experience was one of a one-pointed love of God to the exclusion of all creatures. In this they were clearly influenced by the Christian mystics who had preceded them in the Eastern Christian lands they had overrun. To a modern Christian it may seem strange that these early Christian mystics should think that the love of God must necessarily exclude the love of all creatures, but that they did so is plain enough from their own writings and even more so by their sometimes fanatically anti social behaviour, and this seems to contradict the second great commandment to love your neighbour as yourself. In Islam you do not have quite the same contradiction, since, for the rigidly orthodox, God was so transcendent and so utterly unlike the created order that to speak of loving him was almost blasphemous. Nevertheless, the early Sūfīs were not slow to find texts in the Koran which did speak of the love of God in however attenuated a form. Junayd himself had much to say about love and the torment the soul could experience at the hands of his 'jealous' God; yet when he defines the actual experience of *tawhīd* he speaks not of union (which is actually one of the meanings of the word) but of 'isolation', which would seem to preclude union by definition.

I cannot enter into the reasons for this paradox or discuss Junayd's attempt to resolve it but would simply take note of his definition: 'to isolate the eternal from the originated', which as a statement of the orthodox Muslim position seems unimpeachable but as a description of an experience seems well nigh incomprehensible.

Note again that he speaks of the Eternal simply, not of God or the Truth as the Muslim mystics liked to speak of their God. In Islam this seems strange: and yet it is the best definition I have yet found of the mysticism without love which is in fact typical of one whole stream of Indian religion. In the sense of Junayd's definition Indian religion is mystical through and through: it is not about God (by which I mean an eternal Person operating in time) but about Eternity itself, which is quite beyond and apart from time and space. The essence of the mystical experience is to realise yourself as timeless and eternal or, to put it more concretely in Tennyson's words, to see that 'death is an almost laughable impossibility'. This may be experienced in a variety of ways, or, to oversimplify, there are *two* main ways in which it can be experienced, the way of Junayd, in which eternity is isolated from time, and the purely pantheistic way, in which eternity is experienced as suffusing the temporal so that all transient things are seen to be aspects in some sense of the eternal.

The attraction of mysticism, I suppose, is that it has nothing to do with faith, or hope or charity for that matter, but with a living experience of timeless being and therefore the consciousness of the unreality of death. It does not necessarily have anything to do with God (let alone with the God of the Bible or even the Koran); and it certainly has nothing to do with religious law or dogma, nor, so far as I can see, is it necessarily concerned with morality. Rather, as some extremists would say, it promises you release from time and therefore death; and, if released from time, you will necessarily be released from all that takes place in time. It will, then, free you from *karma*, which is simply the Sanskrit word for 'action' or 'works', and that means from both what you do and leave undone – from your good and evil deeds and their consequences, in other words from all personal responsibility: for the man who has passed beyond time must transcend good and evil (for, as Aristotle says, evil can only be present in things, and in a timeless state there are no 'things').[2] Most non-Christian mystics will tell you that you will have transcended personality too so that there will be no sense of responsibility nor will there be any personal relationships. And – the ultimate paradox – there will be no 'you'. This is as true of the mysticism of isolation as it is of the pantheistic variety.

Let us take the 'isolation' type first, and here we would do well to start with primitive Buddhism, the essence of which is precisely Junayd's 'isolation' of the eternal from the originated, in Buddhist terms the isolation of Nirvāna from Saimsāra. The difference is, of course, that for Junayd the eternal can only be God who alone abides when all things perish; but Nirvāna is not God, and Buddhism is not a theistic religion in the sense that it believes in a God who creates, sustains, and ultimately destroys this universe of place and time. Such a God, even if it were accepted that he exists (as it is in most forms of Hinduism) would still remain irrelevant to what the Buddhists conceive to be the true religious quest which is to have done once and for all with the whole business of coming to be and passing away which conditions our world. There is, then, no salvation *of* the world, only salvation *from* the world. On the one hand there is samsāra, *this* world conditioned by space, time, and causation, the essential qualities of which are impermanence, unsubstantiality (*anattā*, 'nothing has a self'), and therefore unease, anxiety, or anguish: on the other hand there is Nirvāna, which means the total transcendence of all this in a state of timeless rapture which has often been compared to St Paul's 'peace which passes all understanding'.

That such a state exists is not considered to be a matter of faith. Given favourable conditions any human being can attain it: it is called not only Nirvāna, which means the 'blowing out' of the flame of desire or craving, but also unmoving or immutable joy. There can be no question of a Christian *unio mystica* since

No uniting ≿ God because
No God

there is no God with whom the soul can unite, and no soul in the Christian sense of that word that can unite with anything. All that you can say is that there is 'something released in what is (always) released (and free)'.[3]

Early Buddhism, like Zen, refuses to be drawn into any metaphysical discussion on the nature of this state of perfect peace and freedom which it calls Nirvana: and in this respect it seems to me that the Buddha was extremely prudent. One thing, however, these early texts repeat time and again, and this is that it is, from their point of view, totally wrong to think of any sort of personal survival in the state of Nirvāna because in the Buddhist scheme of things there is no such thing as a person: there is no 'I' and therefore no 'mine'. You and I are simply bundles of material forms, sensations, perceptions, habits, and consciousness which have no central core which is identifiable as a self. Now mysticism in practically all its shapes and forms teaches that the mystical state (*any* mystical state) requires the taming, suppressing, or even the total destruction of the 'ego', or the empirical self if you prefer it. So in Christianity total love means the total sacrifice of self or in Paul's word the 'death' of the old Adam. That this total death is held to prelude a rebirth in a different form of existence cannot detain us for the moment except that it is perhaps worth pointing out that such imagery would be wholly inappropriate in a Buddhist setting. For the Buddhists, along with the Hindus, believe in a perpetual process of rebirth and redeath and it is precisely from this endless round of coming to be and passing away that release is sought. That you may be reborn in a higher form of existence is fully taken into account but is brushed aside as being rather vulgar. Even if you are reborn as a god your days as a god are still numbered, and once your store of merit has been exhausted you will be reborn again probably here on earth. Birth and death are the very hallmark of earthly existence and are simply the two fruits of Māra, the Buddhist equivalent of the Prince of this ego World, whose name means death but whose essence is desire which, by producing *mortal* life *eo ipso* produces death (*mors*). Hence to be reborn in any form of existence is still to remain in the sphere of samsāra (what Junayd called the 'originated') and still to be no nearer Nirvana where there is neither birth nor death nor becoming of any kind. Hence it is only natural that the Buddha should not talk in terms of rebirth but rather in terms of the non-existence of a personal ego.

We all talk about a 'selfless' man and we have a fairly clear picture of what we mean: but the Buddha went further and simply assured his disciples that nothing that they thought of as this 'self' had any enduring existence. It was not then a question of suppressing, denying, or annihilating your ego which would enable you to taste eternity but one of realising that such an entity has no real existence. The phenomenal you does not exist, or, if you prefer it in English, you are not what you seem (Greek *phainomenon*).

Well, you may ask, what am I? To this the Buddha gave no clear answer, and he was probably right since there is none. But the nature of *experience* of Nirvāna is scarcely in doubt: it is simply Junayd's 'isolation of the eternal from the originated'. You think of yourself as a person sitting at home and reading this book or more generally as someone who was born and will in all probability die. But you are wrong: this is simply the phenomenal you, what you *seem* to be: the real you is simply some thing or other that is free in an atmosphere of unconditioned freedom which has nothing to do with, has totally broken loose from, this world of life and death, love, hate, pleasure and pain. As to God, forget about him since he is probably, the Buddhists thought, no more than a Hindu invention. And the same goes for the Hindu Absolute too. For Buddhist enlightenment (more literally 'being fully awake') means neither union with a personal God nor absorption into an impersonal Absolute, certainly it does not mean realising one's identity with the Absolute One as so many Hindus taught and our own Parmenides implied.

Given then that the essence of the Buddhist experience is to realise timeless, unmoving eternity in oneself, how does one explain such an experience? If we are wise like the Buddha, we will probably not attempt to do so, but many of the Hindus were not wise in this sense, for the mysticism they developed was not shaped by the genius of one man as the Buddhist variety seems to have been. It developed in what could justly be called a pagan society between, say, the years 1000 and 350 BC, and crystallised into an extremely heterogeneous collection of texts known as the Upanishads which are held to be sacred and authoritative by all subsequent Hindu mystical thinkers.

Early Buddhist mysticism is essentially atheistic or, if you prefer it, non-theistic, as little interested in the 'ground' of the universe so dear to the Rhenish Christian mystics as it was in the more conventional God who behaves in such an extraordinary way in the sacred books of the Jews, Christians, and Muslims. Hinduism, on the other hand, was from the beginning interested in the problem of Being and its relationship, if any, to becoming. And in this respect the Upanishads might be compared to the Presocratics in Greece but with this difference: the Presocratics do at least write under their own names and advance their own individual theories whereas the Upanishads present us with what appears to be a hotchpotch of Presocratic ideas in which distinctions are rarely made between what in Greece would be, say, the pure monism of Parmenides on the one hand and the union of opposites championed by Heraclitus.

If the Buddha's prime concern was the isolation of the eternal from the originated, then we might say that the authors of the Upanishads were obsessed with the problem of the One and the many. In general it can be said that the earlier texts see the Eternal in and through the temporal, or, in their terms, the One in and through the many, while a later trend is to see the One only as being what they call the 'Real of the real'[4] and the many as in some sense illusory.

This is what is usually called pantheism: in one of my books I described it rather as 'pan-en-henism'[5]– 'all-in-one-ness' so as not to prejudge the issue by introducing the Greek word for God into the definition. In the Upanishads the word for a personal god is *deva* (cf. Latin *deus*) but this is rejected out of hand once they had arrived at the idea of an Absolute which is the unchanging ground of the universe, for none of the traditional gods of mythology fitted this bill at all. The words they used were 'Brahman' and 'Ātman' which originally meant 'sacred power' and 'self' respectively, hence the all-pervading sacred spirit which sustains the universe without and the innermost essence of individual men. The essence of the teaching of the Upanishads is usually considered to be the total identification of the two: man's inmost soul is identical with the World Soul or, if you prefer it, with the Holy Spirit, the one member of the Christian Trinity which, *pace* the theologians, is manifestly not a person (for to call 'breath' (*spiritus*) a person seems to be palpably absurd). This identity of microcosm and macrocosm is perhaps best expressed in *Chāndogya Upanishad* 8.1.1–5:

> Now, in this city of Brahman there is a dwelling-place, a tiny lotus-flower: within that there is a tiny space. What is within that is what you should seek: that is what you should really want to understand.
>
> If [his pupils] should say to him: 'Granted that there is a dwelling-place, a tiny lotus-flower, within this city of Brahman, and that within that there is a tiny space, what, then, is to be found there that we should seek out and really want to understand?'
>
> Then he should say: 'As wide as is this space around us, so wide is this space within the heart. In it both sky and earth are concentrated, both fire and wind, both sun and moon, lightning and the stars, what a man possesses here on earth and what he does not possess: everything is concentrated in this [tiny space within the heart].'
>
> If they should say to him: 'If all this is concentrated within this city of Brahman – all beings and all desires – what is left of it all when old age overtakes it and it falls apart?'
>
> Then should he say: 'It does not grow old with [the body's] ageing nor is it slain when [the body] is slain. This is the true city of Brahman: in it are concentrated all desires. This is the Self, exempt from evil, untouched by age or death or sorrow, untouched by hunger or thirst: [this is the Self] whose desire is the real, whose idea is the real.'

What does this mean? It means simply that the true essence of man *is* Brahman, the ground of the universe, and that when you finally die you realise this identity, you are merged into the eternal ground of all things as a drop of water or a river merges into the sea: you live not as an individual any more but with the life of the source of all contingent beings and thereby with the whole universe. In this sense you can say: 'I *am* this whole universe.' Unlike the early Buddhist *separation* of spirit from matter, there is a complete fusion of the two and you, no longer an individual, live with the life of the entire universe. You as an individual are melted or liquefied (mysticism of all religions uses this particular analogy); and being liquefied you are thereby liquidated (after all, what is there in a suffix?).

So much for the pan-en-henic experience of fusion. Let us now turn to a second Upanishadic theme – that of sleep. In the European tradition it has always been assumed that to be awake is a more satisfactory because a more fully conscious condition than being asleep (who would want to be like the ever-sleeping Endymion? Aristotle contemptuously asks).[6] Quite the reverse is true in the Upanishads, for, after all, in our own tradition too, final beatitude is spoken of as *requies aeterna* ('eternal rest'). Dream, then, is better than being awake, because when you are awake you are unavoidably conditioned by the outside world: hence you are obviously not free, and the words the Buddhists and Hindus use for 'salvation' mean 'liberation' or 'freedom', and freedom means total independence of anything else, what the Greeks call *autarkeia*, total self-sufficiency. In dreaming at least you are partially free since you are no longer conscious of the outside world but *create* your own 'outside' world: the dreamer and what he dreams are in a sense one, but not wholly one since the dreamer cannot his dream – he may indeed himself be the victim of horrible nightmares. Hence, a greater degree of reality must be represented by deep, dreamless sleep because this is the most unified state we can reach in this life. Finally to become one means to die, and this is true freedom, for in death all things become absolutely one and nothing can therefore affect this unified being since, so far as he is concerned, nothing else exists that could interfere with his perfect autarky. But there is a snag, and, as one of the Upanishads puts it: 'Such a man, it seems to me, has no present knowledge of himself (or the Self) so that he could say: "This I am", nor, for that matter, has he any knowledge of those creatures here. Surely he might as well be a man annihilated. I see nothing enjoyable in this.'[7]

A little mundane perhaps, but one sees the point. If the total unconsciousness of dreamless sleep is the nearest we can get to what all mystics of whatever persuasion describe as absolute bliss, then will not this absolute bliss be realised in death itself, that is eternal stillness and repose? The answer supplied by both the Upanishads and the early Buddhists would appear to be Yes. So too the Zen Buddhists speak of the Great Death – 'die while yet alive and be completely dead', or, as a Sufi tradition puts it, 'Die before you die'. We find the same view expressed far nearer home by no less a person than Plato. 'Most people', he writes, 'are unaware that those who are seriously engaged in the pursuit of philosophy are really studying nothing but dying and being dead. If, then, this is true, it would be absurd to spend one's whole life in devotion to this alone and then be upset when it comes.'[8]

What, then, is this bliss which death brings? One of the later Upanishads supplies the answer, for beyond the tranquil bliss of dreamless sleep there is a yet more profound bliss in which all duality is finally transcended:

> Conscious of neither within nor without, nor of both together, not a mass of wisdom, neither wise nor unwise, unseen, one with whom there is no commerce, impalpable, devoid of distinguishing mark, unthinkable, indescribable, its essence the firm conviction of the oneness of itself, bringing all development to an end, tranquil and mild, devoid of duality, such do they deem this fourth state [beyond dreamless sleep] to be. That is the Self: that is what should be known.[9]

This in fact is the Absolute, the One which alone is. Obviously if you can realise yourself as actually *being* the Absolute, this must be the final goal beyond which it is impossible to go. The Hindu monists were not slow to draw the obvious conclusion. If the human soul *is* the Absolute One, then all plurality must be an illusion and at the summit of this illusory pyramid stands God, the creator and sustainer of the phenomenal universe: an illusory God deluding his illusory self into the belief that he is the Lord who holds supreme power over an illusory world. If, then, the world and God are from the absolute point of view illusory, then it plainly can make no difference what goes on in this world: all opposites are identical and the opposites of course include good and evil. In other words, as the Upanishads and the *Bhagavad-Gītā* never tire of telling us, the liberated self which has realised itself as the Absolute Self has necessarily transcended good and evil. God, together with his commands and prohibitions is therefore pure make-believe, and what you do (your *karma*) is seen to be of no consequence because it simply does not exist.

However, this experience of absolute oneness can be differently interpreted. Does it necessarily mean the absolute oneness of the

Absolute or does it not rather mean the basic oneness of each human soul as it exists in eternity? This problem too is not foreign to Western thought.

In his *De Anima*[12] Aristotle speaks of a mysterious entity called the *poietikos nous* which alone survives physical death, while in the *Metaphysics* he speaks of the Absolute as the Unmoved Mover[13] or the 'thinking of thought'[10]. Are the two entities the same or different? Of the Muslim commentators on Aristotle Avicenna maintained that they were different, human eternal souls being dependent on the Unmoved Mover like everything else, whereas Averroës maintained that they were identical.

Similarly in India the Sānkaya school of philosophy maintained that there was an infinity of human souls and that the experience of unfractionable oneness meant no more than the realisation of one's own eternal being as utterly distinct from matter and all that depends on it, including mind, the ego and what we call soul. Whichever way you interpret the experience, the experience itself is the same, the *isolation* of the eternal from the originated, as Junayd had said. In neither case is there any room for God as a separate *real* entity. And so, as you would expect, there *is* no God in the Sānkhya system. Nor is there or can there be any room for love since love necessarily assumes duality and in the One this is impossible: nor can there be love between totally isolated timeless spiritual monads, for love would destroy their total isolation and self-sufficiency.

Leaving philosophical interpretations aside, it can be affirmed that the mysticism of isolation assumes two totally distinct forms of existence, pure being which is beyond space and time, and the phenomenal world which depends on both. In the later Upanishads a new idea appears (as it appears in the later philosophical Muslim mystics) and that is that there is in fact a Supreme Being who transcends eternity as much as he transcends time. The crucial verse is this:

> In the imperishable, infinite city of Brahman
> > Two things there are –
> Wisdom and unwisdom, hidden, established there:
> Perishable is unwisdom, but wisdom is immortal:
> Who over wisdom and unwisdom rules, He is Another.[11]

This other is the ancient god Rudra-Shiva who now for the first time appears as God with a capital G. It is at this stage that love between the soul and God not only becomes philosophically possible but also develops like wildfire until it becomes a sensuously passionate affair which all Christian mystics, with their intense preoccupation with the *Song of Songs* would readily have understood. However love is not the subject of this chapter, so we would do well to stop here.

Chapter 3

The Wickedness of Evil

Dietrich Bonhoeffer wrote in 1942:

> 'The great masquerade of evil has played havoc with all our ethical concepts. For evil to appear disguised as light, charity, historical necessity, or social justice is quite bewildering to anyone brought up on our traditional ethical concepts, while for the Christian who bases his life on the Bible it merely confirms the fundamental wickedness of evil. . . .'[1]

'Evil' and, even more, Bonhoeffer's term 'the wickedness of evil' have a very old-fashioned ring nowadays, particularly among those of us who are engaged in the interesting and, I am afraid, fashionable study of comparative religion, the history of religion, *Religionswissenschaft* or whatever you wish to call it. For both 'evil' and especially 'sin' have come to be regarded as Judaeo-Christian taboos designed to exclude from our experience a whole range of liberating activities which (it is alleged) lie at the heart of the mystical religions of the East. Morality, on the whole, seems to be out – while ecstasy is very much 'in': with the result that most of us no longer feel we have a fixed frame of reference from which we can begin to make any sense of our lives. Traditional Christianity as taught by the Churches no longer seems to make any sense. The new theologies are, if anything, more barren than the old: the Mystic East has been called in to redress the 'over-rational' imbalance of the West, and as the French novelist Georges Bernanos said, 'we find ourselves in an indeterminate sphere, among the stones and the rafters, in the rain. . . .' Or to quote Bonhoeffer again:

> 'One may even ask whether there have ever before in human history been people with so little ground under their feet – people to whom every available alternative seemed equally

intolerable, repugnant, and futile.' But he also adds (and
perhaps he is right): 'Or perhaps one should ask whether the
responsible thinking people of any generation that stood at a
turning-point in history did not feel much as we do, simply
because something new was emerging that could not be seen
in the existing alternatives.'

In the field of religion we now have (very roughly) two existing
alternatives. On the one hand we have Christianity which, though
diminished in every way, cannot simply be written off just yet
with the glib serenity with which so many humanists would
gladly dismiss it. On the other, we have the upsurge of Eastern
mysticism which seems to have bewitched the minds of so many
of the young. Between the two there is a gulf fixed with the
result that neither seems to have the slightest idea of what the
other is talking about. It would seem to me that the only factor
the two have in common is an equal dislike and distrust of
human reason. Between the two the obvious bridge is, I suppose,
Teilhard de Chardin, who has reinterpreted Christianity along
mystical and evolutionary lines. Teilhard has, of course, been
criticised on the Christian side for his apparent disregard of the
fundamental Christian dogma of original sin; but the criticism
should go deeper. For what he is by-passing is not so much
original sin (which can very well be interpreted in evolutionary
terms) but what Bonhoeffer called the essential '*wickedness* of
evil'. Let us then dispose of him first.
During the Second World War most of us (including
Bonhoeffer who paid for his convictions with his life) considered
that Hitler represented something so evil that even war was
justified if his tyranny were to be scotched. Not so Teilhard.
'Just now,' he wrote:

'the Germans deserve to win because, however bad or mixed
is their spirit, they have more spirit than the rest of the world.
It is easy to criticise and despise the fifth column. But no
spiritual aim or energy will ever succeed, or even deserve to
succeed, unless it proves able to spread and keep spreading a
fifth column.'[2]

This one quotation must suffice and I will spare the reader

his scientific-progressive dithyrambs on the subject of the atom bomb. In any case I cannot myself reconcile this worship of progress for its own sake with Christianity in any hitherto known form. This seems to go a very long way beyond rendering unto Caesar the things that are Caesar's and appears to uphold with considerable vigour the doctrine that might is right. In the West this doctrine has hitherto found little favour since it was castigated by Plato – a Greek, one should remember, not a Jew. And perhaps one ought also to be reminded at this stage that Western civilisation as we know it has been far more Graeco-Roman than Judaeo-Christian. Its father, I sometimes like to think, was not so much 'Jesus the Jew' as Aristotle, the Greek, who tried to think his way from time to eternity without those messy Platonic short cuts.

Teilhard's bridge, it seems to me, is an irrational bridge between one form of unreason and another, between, one might add, one form of amorality and another.

In his last months in prison Bonhoeffer had plenty of time to reflect, and much of this time he spent in reading the Bible and particularly the Old Testament, a document large portions of which I was made to read at school with the results one might expect. For it seemed to me that here was a book that seemed to condone everything that I was supposed to think wicked. This did not escape the imprisoned Bonhoeffer either though he at least could read the text with the eye of faith: he could discern the goodness of God through the apparent wickedness of his commands to his chosen few.

'Why is it', he wistfully asks, 'that in the Old Testament men tell lies vigorously and often to the glory of God (I've now collected the passages), kill, deceive, rob, divorce, and even fornicate . . . doubt, blaspheme, and curse, whereas in the New Testament there is nothing of all this? "An earlier stage" of religion? That is a very naïve way out; it is one and the same God.'[3]

Yes, it *is* one and the same God and he is the God of the Koran *and* the Bhagavad-Gītā too. It is the same God whom Jung analysed in his little book *Answer to Job* and his conclusion was the same: not only does God condone and even encourage wickedness in man, he is himself wicked or, at least, amoral.

The Book of Job is a landmark in the long historical development of the divine drama. At the time the book was written, there were already many testimonies which had given a contradictory picture of Yahweh – the picture of a God who knew no moderation in his emotions and suffered precisely from this lack of moderation. He himself admitted that he was eaten up with rage and jealousy and that this knowledge was painful to him. Insight existed along with obtuseness, loving-kindness along with cruelty, creative power along with destructiveness. Everything was there, and none of these qualities was an obstacle to the other. Such a condition is only thinkable either when no reflecting consciousness is present at all, or when the capacity for reflection is very feeble and a more or less adventitious phenomenon. A condition of this sort can only be described as *amoral*. psychotic

I shall not give a cool and carefully considered exegesis that tries to be fair to every detail, but a purely subjective reaction. In this way I hope to act as a voice for many who feel the same way as I do, and to give expression to the shattering emotion that the unvarnished spectacle of divine savagery and ruthlessness produces in us.[4]

paranoia

Now, you cannot have been Professor of Eastern Religions and Ethics for some twenty years without fully agreeing with what Jung says; and you cannot fail to understand how anyone brought up in the more gentle ways of Buddhism, for instance, must be revolted by this savage God who, whatever he may demand of men, wantonly and wilfully himself violates every precept the gentle Buddha had taught. The Buddha did not believe in a creator God, and this is one of the reasons, I think, that so many young people are turning to Buddhism today. If indeed there *is* a creator God and he has indeed *revealed* himself in the Bible and the Koran, then, the Buddhist would surely say, the less we know about him the better: to us he seems much more like Māra, the Buddha's eternal enemy who keeps the world in being only to prolong forever human misery and suffering.

And what again are we to make of a God who commands Joshua to put all the inhabitants of Jericho, men, women and children, to the sword – not to mention the oxen and donkeys,[5] or his even more emphatic command to Saul to deal likewise with the Amalekites: 'Do not spare them, but kill man and

"< Desire > o Death

woman, babe and suckling, ox and sheep, camel and donkey.'[6] Saul demurs, and is driven mad for his pains or as Scripture puts it, 'an evil spirit from Yahweh filled him with terror'. Today we would call this genocide, in this case divinely commanded genocide. Does then the wickedness of evil reside in the very heart of God? And in God is might after all right? To judge from God's own answer to Job we have no alternative but to say 'yes', since God's only answer is that *because* he is omnipotent he must be obeyed, however capricious, however crazy he may show himself to be. Who else but he could claim worship *because* he had made so stupid and careless a creature as the ostrich 'cruel to her chicks as if they were not hers', for 'God, you see, has made her unwise, and given her no share of common sense'.[7] Job is simply cowed into submission by a display of brute, irrational force, the force of the creator, of evil as well as good, as he himself admits.[8]

As Jung puts it, Job 'clearly sees that God is at odds with himself – so totally at odds that he, Job, is quite certain of finding in God a helper and an "advocate" against God. As certain as he is of the evil in Yahweh, he is equally certain of the good. In a human being who renders us evil we cannot expect at the same time to find a helper. But Yahweh is not a human being: he is both a persecutor and a helper in one, and the one aspect is as real as the other. Yahweh is not split but is an *antinomy* – a totality of inner opposites – and this is the indispensable condition of his tremendous dynamism.'[9] How, then, can we call him good? In purely human terms we cannot, not even in the terms of our present-day relative moralism which tends to fight shy of any moral or value judgement whatever. Most people still draw the line at genocide, and that is exactly what Yahweh demanded of Joshua and Saul. But then you cannot argue with this God, for, as he himself says: 'My thoughts are not your thoughts, my ways are not your ways . . . Yes, the heavens are as high above the earth as my ways are above your ways, my thoughts above your thoughts.'[10] Yes, this is the 'totally other' all right, but nobody takes him seriously any more. Many have turned for more mystical comfort to the East. And what have they found there?

What they have found, it seems to me, is that religion does not necessarily mean an unquestioning obedience to the will of

Someone who, to the average man of today, must appear as an irrational and sometimes brutal tyrant: indeed the very existence of such a supreme being can be brushed aside as altogether unnecessary as was done by the Buddha. Better still, it may also mean that the moral code which this apparently amoral God lays down for men can, in higher states of religious consciousness, be seen to be purely relative. The good of man, then, will no longer be to carry out the commandments of a God who now seems not only unreasonable but also totally outmoded but to enter into a state of being in which both the whole relative order and the God who is supposed to support and transcend it are themselves transcended in 'that which is neither born nor made, neither comes to be nor is compounded',[11] as the Buddha once described this ineffable state which he called Nirvana. In addition both the Buddhists and the Hindus assure us that this is a state that can be reached here and now in this life: in life itself we can transcend life and all its sufferings and contradictions: we can experience ourselves as immortal and free, 'like gods', beyond good and evil. Admittedly, the classical texts of Hinduism and Buddhism offer us little hope that we can achieve this sublime condition in this life but will probably have to endure countless reincarnations before we achieve our goal.

However, never mind. What with the development of modern science and technology it appears that the same ineffable ecstasies can be obtained by the use of drugs or better still by the 'easy way' of Transcendental Meditation obtainable from the Maharishi Mahesh Yogi and other widely advertised gurus. And this is after all what so many young people are looking for today. Religion, they feel, is not really a matter of duty or belief or even of social service and a compassionate love of your fellow man but of direct experience of the Divine. This the churches no longer supply if they ever did: hence the rush to oriental mysticism with its promise of an experience of eternity here and now. That ecstasy is desirable is taken for granted, no matter what its content and consequences may be. Hitherto in the West ecstasy has been very much a hit and miss affair: it simply happened (if it happened at all); it came and went like a flash of lightning, leaving you with a sense of absolute certainty and absolute reality behind. Typical of this kind of ecstasy was that experienced by the Canadian doctor, R. M. Bucke, who has left us an account of his experience and his interpretation of it. It lasted only three minutes but in those three minutes he reached conclusions about the 'true' nature of the universe which never left him. He described the nature of the experience as 'Cosmic Consciousness' and held that only such experiences could account for the original impetus at the source of *all* religions:

'This (Cosmic) Consciousness (or "Brahmic Splendour")', he wrote, 'shows the cosmos to consist not of dead matter governed by unconscious, rigid, and unintending law; it shows it on the contrary as entirely immaterial, entirely spiritual and entirely alive; it shows that death is an absurdity, that everyone and everything has eternal life; it shows that the universe is God and that God is the universe, and that no evil ever did or ever will enter into it.'[12]

'Cosmic Consciousness', he calls it, or 'Brahmic bliss', which shows that he must have been conversant with the sacred scriptures of the Hindus. It shows that death is an absurdity and that evil does not really exist. The whole thing was long ago put into a nutshell in the *Katha* Upanishad (2.19) in these memorable words:

> Should the killer think: 'I kill',
> Or the killed, 'I have been killed',
> Both these have no right knowledge:
> He kills not, is not killed.

The logic of both Bucke and the Upanishad seems to me impeccable. In 'Cosmic Consciousness' you pass clean beyond individual existence and live with the life of the whole universe which cannot die; you have realised a 'timeless moment', an 'eternal Now', as the Neo-Platonists put it, from the vantage point of which all action, whether good or evil, must seem ultimately illusory. Here there is no distinction between killing and being killed: you have passed beyond right and wrong, good and evil. Hence you may arrive at the equally dangerous dictum of St Augustine, 'Love and do what you will.'

This moral relativism runs like a quicksilver thread throughout all Hinduism, and it is against this that the Buddha reacted. *He* at least was only too conscious of the reality of evil, identifying it as he did with transience. For him salvation meant release from the impermanence of this world into an eternal state of being, the eternal 'Now' if you like, but in order to reach this state, he maintained, you must first master the basic moral commandments – do not kill, do not fornicate, do not steal, do not lie, do not envy – all interpreted much as Jesus interpreted the corresponding commandments in the Decalogue: to reach the deathless you must first be good, that is, totally un-self-regarding.

However, there is always the Devil to be reckoned with, and the Buddha had distinct views on the Devil, though not Zoroastro-Christian ones to which I myself incline. According to the Zoroastrians, closely followed by St John, the principal characteristics of the Devil are that he is a murderer, a liar, and a deceiver. To corrupt and distort every religion in the interests of the 'wickedness of evil' is his dearest concern. As Bernanos puts it: 'He is in the prayer of the hermit, in his fasts and penances, at the heart of the deepest ecstasy, and in the silence of the heart. He poisons holy water, burns in the consecrated wax, breathes in the breath of virgins . . . corrupts every religious way.'[13] 'Corrupts every religious way': that is about it. He makes us blind to the 'wickedness of evil' in Buddhism just as much as in Judaism and Christianity. In Buddhism the case was perhaps more difficult since there is no omnipotent God who in the last analysis must himself, though good, have created evil for reasons we cannot understand and he does not explain. But in Buddhism there is no such God and the Buddha has shown the infallible way – the hard way – that leads from moral goodness to enlightenment and eternal peace.

But Buddhism developed, as religions do, and it was not the original teachings of the Buddha that made any real impact on the West but its very late Zen variety as transmitted by the late Dr Suzuki and his American acolytes, who pointed out that in Nirvana there is 'neither production nor annihilation, neither coming nor going, *neither right nor wrong*'.[14] We have reached the thin end of the wedge: the Devil's appetite has been whetted. More is to come, for an English lady, the Venerable Jiyu Kennett, Abbess of Shasta Abbey, California, has now gone so far as to say: 'It is as bad to keep the Precepts out of attachment to morality as it is not to keep them at all; it is good to break them in order to teach the immorality of morality to those still suffering from attachment to morality.'[15] The Devil licks his chops. We seem to be back to the non-existence of killer and killed in the eternal Now.

For most of its modern enthusiasts Eastern mysticism means either Zen or Neo-Vedanta, non-dualism as it is frequently called. This Aldous Huxley has called the 'perennial philosophy', and at its heart lies the 'coincidence of opposites' so dear to the heart of C. G. Jung. In the Absolute One all the opposites are fused into One, and evil is seen simply as an aspect of good: 'justice *is* strife,' as our own Heraclitus said. Or, in the words of Charles Manson, whom we shall be discussing later: 'If God is One, what is bad?'[16] R. M. Bucke, the idealist Canadian doctor and Charles Manson, the unruffled murderer and master of murderers: curious company, you may think. Perhaps, but behind them lies an ancient Hindu tradition as old as the Upanishads and the Bhagavad-Gītā.

Early Buddhism did not recognise a creator God nor did it formally admit even an impersonal Absolute. In both respects it seems to have been reacting against the contemporary trend in Hinduism which roundly affirmed the Absolute which it called Brahman or alternatively the supreme self. For the strict non-dualist only the Absolute – the Absolute One – really existed: therefore from the absolute point of view all that takes place in space and time must be an illusion. Hence man's supreme good is to realise himself as the Absolute, but to achieve this absolute point of view two stages must first be traversed. First the everyday 'ego' must be suppressed; secondly it must be replaced by the absolute Self (which is the real you). Only when this is achieved can the identity of all changing things in the changeless One be realised – a One in which there is no difference at all. In Hindu terms this realisation of the Self-Absolute-All necessarily means release from all bondage to works, or, if you prefer it in Sanskrit, to *karma*, a concept with which Charles Manson was quite familiar. By transcending *karma*, of course, you transcend good and evil, and about this the early Hindu texts, unlike their Buddhist counterparts, make no bones at all. Whether Charles Manson had direct access to these original texts or not I do not know; but that his 'philosophy' was largely based on them as filtered down to him by the various semi-Oriental sects with which he was in contact in the Los Angeles area seems fairly

non-moral duality

certain. As typical of these texts we may quote the following
from the Upanishads: *breath - garment (self)*
                                making

> That from which all words recoil together with the mind,
>   Unable to attain it –
> That is the bliss of Brahman; knowing it,
> A man has nothing to fear from anywhere.
>
> Such a man is not worried by the thought:
> 'Why did I not do good? Why did I do evil?'
> Knowing good and evil in this way he saves himself:
> Who knows them both as such, he saves himself.
> Such is the secret teaching.[17]

Or, more striking still:

> But Indra did not swerve from the truth, for Indra *is* truth.
> So he said:

> Know me, then, as I am. This indeed is what I consider
> most beneficial to mankind – that they should know me. I
> killed the three-headed son of Tvashtri, I threw the
> Arunmukhna ascetics to the hyenas. Transgressing many a
> compact, I impaled the people of Prahlāda on the sky, the
> Paulomas on the atmosphere and the Kālakānjas on the earth,
> and I did not lose a single hair in the process.
>   The man who knows me as I am loses nothing that is his,
> whatever he does, even though he should slay his mother or
> father, even though he should steal or procure an abortion.
> Whatever evil he does, he does not blanch.[18]

treaty
carta

Charles Manson did *not* blanch, and in this he was faithful to
a very ancient and very venerable Indian tradition. From the
same tradition he learnt to accept the doctrine of reincarnation
and the law of *Karma*. On how this should be interpreted the
Bhagavad-Gītā (2. 18–9) is very clear indeed: 'Finite, they say,
are these our bodies indwelt by an eternal embodied self . . .
Fight then, scion of Bharata. Who thinks this self can be a killer,
who thinks that it can be killed, both these have no right knowledge:
it does not kill nor is it killed.'
  In other words, on the absolute plane, where there is no time,

there can be neither birth nor death: both are equally illusory and therefore meaningless; and if birth and death are meaningless, then reincarnation itself must be meaningless and an illusion. And so the Gita (2.26) adds: 'And even if you think that [the soul] is constantly reborn and constantly re-dies, even so you grieve for it in vain. For sure is the death of all that is born, sure is the birth of all that dies: so in a matter that no one can prevent you have no cause to grieve'.

On the absolute plane, then, killing and being killed are equally unreal, but on the relative plane the law of *Karma*, the natural and moral law which predetermines our next incarnation according to the deeds we have done during this life, still holds sway. *But* the whole point of the Gita is to persuade Arjuna to fight in an admittedly just war the 'kill-count' of which was to reach what must be a record total of 1,660,020,000 dead. Arjuna does not like this idea, but Krishna, the incarnate God, persuades him that once he has reached the absolute state of Brahman which manifests itself as a total detachment from all earthly things and all earthly deeds, whether good or evil, he can no longer be affected by them. He will be like a god, exempt alike from exultation and remorse. He does not mince his words: 'A man who has reached a state where there is no sense of "I", whose soul is undefiled – were he to slaughter all these worlds – slays nothing. He is not bound.'[19]

In other words, the text seems to say, once you have truly got rid of all sense of ego, you will find that you can murder to your heart's content and feel no remorse at all: you will have passed beyond good and evil.

These are the kind of doctrines that percolated through to Charles Manson and his acolytes, and, with perfect logic, they acted on them. What shocked the world when they were caught and brought to trial was that none of them showed any sign of remorse. This is not surprising, for, in the jargon of the Manson family, they had reached 'Now' – the eternal Now of the Neo-Platonists: they had passed beyond time and therefore beyond good and evil. How had this come about? The accepted explanation is that it was all due to LSD. But this is too facile. LSD does produce changed and expanded forms of consciousness, and there have been cases when it has led to suicide, but it does not normally lead to deliberate, callous murder. Of course Charles

Manson used both LSD and 'ultra-sex' to produce ecstatic states in his female acolytes, but this does not alone explain how he succeeded in destroying both his own and their consciences, the uncanny hold he had over them, and the serene ruthlessness with which he was prepared to kill human beings, some of whom were total strangers to him. The explanation would appear to be threefold: (i) he had what seems to have been a classic 'enlightenment' experience, (ii) he had been in constant conflict with society since his earliest years, and (iii) in addition he came to identify himself with the Christ of the Book of Revelation. These three facts between them account for Manson's rather peculiar spiritual development.

The end and goal of both Hinduism and Buddhism is to pass into a form of existence in which time and space and all the opposites that bedevil human existence are totally transcended and in which one is literally 'dead' to the world but alive in a timeless eternity. This ritual death Charles Manson had already experienced, and, as a result of this experience, he had taught his disciples that they must kill themselves in this way in order to kill others and be free from remorse. At the trial when Linda Kasabian, who had witnessed the ecstatic massacre of Sharon Tate and her associates but was not sufficiently de-ego-ised to participate, appeared as the principal witness for the prosecution, Susan Atkins, the most egoless of them all, 'mouthed the words, "You're killing us." To which Linda replied in a whisper quite audible to the jury' – and, it may be added, in a language that made perfect sense to Charlie – ' "I'm not killing you. You've killed yourselves." ' She had heard it so often before. 'Yes,' she said again in that interminable cross-examination, 'he used to say "If you are willing to be killed, then you should be willing to kill." '[20] Charles Manson *had* killed himself, but at the trial he had come to life again not as a superman or a god but as a very human being, the son of a teenage prostitute, a 'country boy who never grew up', as he once described himself.

The whole mystical business had started when he was very young. Then

. . . he suddenly felt that he was as powerful and free as Superman. He acquired a makeshift cloak, climbed up to the roof, spread his arms and sailed through the air. It was a great feeling, comparable to an orgasm, and one that he never forgot. When Sandy tells it there is the strong implication that Charlie really did fly. No matter. The point here is that the cloak and Superman and the *feeling* are part of the Family's Manson legend.

— memory of all pest places as seeted

Flying at will, it should be noted, was one of the preternatural powers attributed to the Buddha and indeed to all who have achieved enlightenment by his followers. The disciples of C. G. Jung would probably say that flying referred to the perfect freedom the enlightened person enjoys in his own 'inner space'. There is no reason to believe that Charlie did not have this experience. You do not have to be a saint to do that: LSD can do it for you too.

Freedom of the spirit he had, then, already experienced, but not the complete extinction of the ego of which the mystics of all religions perpetually speak. Since he was thoroughly conversant with the Bible he realised that he must be crucified if he were to rise again to eternal life. The ego must die if the true Self or 'Soul' is to be born. Hence he submitted to a ritual crucifixion.

Not far from Spahn ranch the Family discovered an almost secret clearing guarded by a natural surrounding wall of large boulders. On one side of the clearing was a hill, The Hill of Martyrdom. For upon this hilly boulder-shaped secret clearing was performed perhaps the world's first outdoor LSD crucifixion ceremony.

Then they snuffed Charlie, in role as Jesus, strapping (not nailing) him to an actual rustic cross, while others, acting as tormentors and apostles, jeered and weeped.

Charlie's crucifixion symbolised for him the death of his ego. It was, however, still only a symbol. He had not experienced what the Zen Buddhists call the 'Great Death': this he experienced in a 'final flash he received while meditating in the desert'. There seems to be no evidence that the experience was brought on by LSD.

He is reported as saying: 'Once I was walking in the desert and I had a revelation. I'd walked about forty-five miles and that is a lot of miles to walk in a desert. The sun was beating down on me and I was afraid because I wasn't willing to accept death. My tongue swoll up and I could hardly breathe. I collapsed in the sand.

'I looked at the ground and I saw this rock out of the corner of my eye. And I remember thinking in this insane way as I looked at it, "Well, this is as good a place as any to die." '

Then he started to laugh. 'I began laughing like an insane man. I was so happy.' Then he got up 'with ease' and walked ten miles forthwith and reached safety.

Charles Manson had apparently achieved what the Zen Buddhists call enlightenment, the supreme lightning flash which shatters the time barrier, and through which one is reborn in eternity where time does not exist and death is, therefore, as Tennyson said, 'an almost laughable impossibility'. All things are fused into one; *karma* is transcended and, with it, of course, good and evil. This seems to be the essence of Zen *satori*. Plenty of cases of this have been recorded, but one must suffice. It is the experience of a Japanese executive aged forty-seven, and this is how he describes it:

I was now lying on my back. Suddenly I sat up and struck the bed with all my might and beat the floor with my feet, as if trying to smash it, all the while laughing riotously. My wife and youngest son, sleeping near me, were now awake and frightened. Covering my mouth with her hand, my wife exclaimed: 'What's the matter with you? What's the matter with you?' But I wasn't aware of this until told about it afterwards. My son told me later he thought I had gone mad.

'I've come to enlightenment! Shakyamuni and the Patriarchs haven't deceived me! They haven't deceived me!' I remember crying out . . .

That morning I went to see Yasutani-roshi and tried to describe to him my experience of the sudden disintegration of heaven and earth. 'I am overjoyed, I am overjoyed!' I kept repeating. . . . Tears came which I couldn't stop. I tried to relate to him the experience of that night, but my mouth trembled and words wouldn't form themselves. In the end I just put my face in his lap. Patting me on the back, he said:

'Well, well, it is rare indeed to experience to such a wonderful degree. It is termed "Attainment of the emptiness of Mind". You are to be congratulated!'[21]

If this middle-aged Japanese executive is to be congratulated, so is Charles Manson. To my mind there would appear to be little doubt that what he experienced was precisely what the Japanese executive experienced. The secret of Charles Manson is that he *knew* this timeless moment can at least be simulated by LSD and in a 'total' and brutal exercise of the physical sexual act. Lucidly he drew the obvious conclusion which most of our modern Zen Buddhists do all they can to hush up. Where he had been, all things were One and there was 'no diversity at all':[22] he had passed beyond good and evil. At last he was free!

How that Japanese executive used his 'freedom' we are not told. Perhaps he too had a mind as consistently logical as Manson's and, with his greater experience, he may even now be vicariously murdering the innocent citizens of Tokyo. Like Charlie he too had done it the hard way, the way of *zāzen*, 'just sitting' and sitting and sitting until that wicked discursive mind disintegrates and you *see* that right *is* wrong, and good *is* evil. Charlie didn't sit: he walked forty-five miles until he reached the point of exhaustion: he collapsed and *saw*. He saw a rock: but it was no longer an ordinary rock but the 'Uncarved Block' of the Taoists which 'is the symbol of the primal undifferentiated unity underlying the apparent complexity of the universe.'[23]

'The sun was beating down on Charlie.' The sun is hot, and one of the Sanskrit words for heat is *tapas*. But *tapas* also came to mean fierce ascetic practices resulting in the mortification – the making dead – of the mind. There is a *tapas* of sitting – *Zāzen* – and a *tapas* of walking – Charlie's *tapas*. The physical result of all forms of *tapas* is the same. 'Recent physiological investigations of these practices in a laboratory setting tend to confirm the notion that provoked alterations in body chemistry and body rhythm are in no small way responsible for the dramatic changes in consciousness attendant upon these practices.'[24]

All very interesting no doubt. But Charles Manson instinctively knew that what he had experienced in the desert after walking forty-five miles in the blazing sun could also be experienced under LSD and ultra-sex. As he knew so he acted.

The experience provided by Zen seems to be identical with
what R. M. Bucke called Cosmic Consciousness. This is the
second level of consciousness from which Charles Manson acted.
When under the influence of mescaline Aldous Huxley spoke of
'Is-ness', the 'eternal Now' of Meister Eckhart, the medieval
German mystic. Charlie knew all about this too. 'No past – time
burnt – books burnt – past burnt . . . All time factors melted in
the now. The now of Charlie.' The man who, like Charlie, has
achieved Cosmic Consciousness, lives in and from the level of the
Now, but the average mortal who lives in, for, and from ego-
consciousness only, can only find the Now in death. Hence it
was only logical that he should deal in death ('Death is Charlie's
trip,' as Tex Watson, the most devoted and savage of his murder-
squad, laconically and truly observed). And so, when one of his
minor associates, Shorty Shea, showed signs of 'snitching', 'they
got Shorty in his car . . . They hit him in the head with a big
wrench. They took him with them. They let him sweat. When he
would come to, they would cut him some more. He was begging
for his life. They finally had to cut his head off. He got to Now
and they killed him.' Logical enough, you will say, but Charlie
was himself perfectly capable of making distinctions and could
concede that there were occasions on which people were not
ready physically to undergo the supreme experience: 'her ego
wasn't ready to die', he said of Linda Kasabian on one occasion,
an imperfection on her part which was to prove fatal to him.

Once you have reached the stage of the eternal Now, all is
One, as Parmenides taught in ancient Greece. 'After all', Manson
said, 'We are all one.' Killing someone therefore is just like
breaking off a piece of cookie. And did not the Manson adage
say 'If you're willing to be killed you should be willing to kill'?
He was perfectly sincere in this and sometimes would hand his
knife to an adversary, bidding him kill him. The offer was never
accepted, for the Family regarded Charlie as almost divine. This
was his third level of awareness: the crucified ego merges into
the Infinite, transcends Time and *descends* again transfigured
into a 'superego' or 'superman', eternal in essence but operating
in time.

'We are all one' – this is the obverse of the eternal Now.
This whole philosophy was long ago summed up in an ancient
Hindu scripture: 'Whoso thus knows that he is the Absolute,

ego

dionysius frenzie worship
ego inflated
charismatic
ie Alexander
slaughter

becomes this whole universe. Even the gods have not the power to cause him to un-Be, for he becomes their own self.'[25] Or as country Sue, a member of the Family, put it in her more rustic way: 'And like, I'm willing to die for anyone, anyone who's me, 'cause it's like one soul.'

The 'Soul' plays an important part in the Manson ideology. As in Hinduism it is the Absolute both with and without attributes. Without attributes it is the Now of which nothing can be positively predicated; with attributes it is incarnate in Charlie Manson: 'I am Charlie and Charlie is me' is a correct statement of the faith. More elaborately formulated it could be put in this way: 'Charlie is above all wants and desires – he is dead. It isn't Charlie any more. It is the Soul. They are Charlie and Charlie is they.'

All adepts were indeed the Soul in a sense, but Charlie was the Soul absolutely. For you can conceive of this total Soul either as the indwelling spirit that pervades all things or as the controlling genius of all things, what we would call God. As the same Hindu scripture we have quoted above puts it: 'The Soul (*ātman*) is the Lord of all beings, King of all beings. Just as the spokes of a wheel are fixed together on the hub and tyre, so are all beings, all gods, all worlds, all vital breaths and all these selves fixed together in this Soul.'[26] This was precisely Charlie's relationship to the Family: he was their essence and their Lord. Oddly enough Aristotle had precisely the same idea.

'We must consider', he said, 'in which sense the nature of the Whole is the "good" and the "supremely good"; whether it is something separate and existent in its own right or is [a principle of] order; or whether it is both, as with an army. For the "good" of an army consists in its order, and yet it *is* the general or rather it is chiefly the general.'[27]

You could scarcely have a more accurate description of the relationship between Charles Manson and his Family. Its 'good' consisted both in the order that reigned in its ranks and the 'general' who gave it its orders. The difference, of course, is that Aristotle, like the Buddha, also believed in a moral order: he did not believe, as Heraclitus and Empedocles had done before him, and as Charles Manson was to believe long after him, in that ancient Hindu assertion that, seen from the absolute point of view, good and evil, order and disorder, are reconciled in the

One. Believing, Manson acted on his beliefs, and many a 'rich pig' was to meet a gruesome and untimely end because Charles Manson, so far from being mad, seems to have had a lucidly logical mind. He took the ambiguities and ambivalences of Indian religion as transmitted to him seriously but drew conclusions that were the exact opposite of the conclusions conventionally drawn.

For many Charles Manson personifies what Bonhoeffer calls the 'wickedness of evil'. Maybe, but on his own premises he was scarcely illogical. He had won his flash of enlightenment the hard way and he had learnt that in Hindu mysticism and in Zen the enlightened man who has realised himself as the Absolute – what he called the Soul – is beyond good and evil. 'If God is One, what is bad?' he is quoted as saying. And again, as an assiduous student of the Bible, he knew that God had commanded genocide in ancient times and that the Word of God would return in the last days, 'his cloak soaked in blood' and himself designated 'to tread out the wine of Almighty God's fierce anger'.[28] Perhaps he was a little fanciful in identifying himself with this Rider of the Apocalypse. Interpret it as you will. Say with Lucretius if you will: *tantum religio potuit suadere malorum*; or take the Zoroastrian way out and insist that evil is and must be a principle independent of and absolutely hostile to God. Alternatively, if you believe in God at all, you must accept the Jewish paradox in some form and simply admit that the 'wickedness of evil' must somehow proceed from the very heart of God and that what God excuses in himself he hates in us. There is no solution to the mystery unless we can understand these hauntingly cryptic words of the Hindi poet Kabir:

> God is a Thug: and Thuggery's what he has brought to the world!
> Yet how can I live without him, tell me, my motherly friend.
> Who is the husband? Who is the wife of whom?
> Ponder on that in your inmost heart.
> Who is the son? And who is the father of whom?
> Who is it who dies? Who is wracked with torment?
> Says Kabir: 'What of it? I'm pleased with the Thug as he is:
> For once I recognized the Thug, the Thuggery vanished away.'[29]

Chapter 4

Tantum religio potuit suadere malorum

'So powerful has religion been to convince men of evil things.'
The quotation is, of course, from Lucretius (*De Rerum Natura*,
I. 101), and it has a very modern ring. It doesn't matter very
much whether you translate the Latin *religio* as 'religion' or
'superstition'. There is very little difference between the two.
Take the 'superstitious' element out of religion and you are left
with only metaphysics and ethics – and the two together can
scarcely be said to constitute religion. True, what religion *is* has
never been adequately defined; but that it has something to do
with unseen powers and uncanny forces beyond the scope of
reason and therefore of science would until quite recently have
been conceded by all. Religion, one might say, is that which
science cannot understand because it is not something that can
be classified and quantified: it can only be affirmed or denied.
Neither its affirmation nor its denial is subject to Sir Alfred Ayer's
'principle of verification'. It is not a 'thing' nor is it a system of
morals; but it is certainly human. The other animals do not
suffer from this particular plague because they have not the power
to reflect on what Lucretius called the 'nature of things'. They
were not foolish enough to eat of what the Book of Genesis calls
the 'tree of the knowledge of good and evil'. Only man did this
and he has been paying for it ever since.

Man, according to the Koran, the Divine Word made *Book*
according to the Muslims, was appointed vice-regent of the
world by God. But the Man whom God created both in Genesis
and the Koran was not only a pairing animal, a social animal, and
a rational animal as Aristotle, the father of the West, had taught;
he was also a religious animal, and it is against this divine gift of
'religion' that Western man has been revolting ever since natural
philosophy snapped its links with religion in ancient Greece.

(margin notes: curiosity ? intelligence | good-desire & evil? kill)

Apparently in vain; for man is not merely a thinking animal in which he is distinguished from the rest of the brute creation, he is also a sexual and aggressive animal in both of which respects he far exceeds the other animals simply *because* he has the gift of reason and can therefore organise both his sexuality and his aggressive drives with ruthless productive and counterproductive efficiency. In addition to all this, insofar as he is a religious animal, he is not only 'like God' but also like the Devil, made in the image of the latter quite as much as he is in that of the former. As a Muslim tradition has it, 'Satan courses through his veins.' The whole situation seen in this way seems to me to be adequately summed up in this verse of the Koran (33.72):

> We offered the trusteeship to the heavens and the earth and the mountains, but they refused to bear it and shrank from it, but man bore it. Surely he is exceedingly unjust and foolish.

On which the Persian mystic Bāyazīd of Bastām ruefully comments: 'O God, you created these people without their knowledge and invested them with trusteeship [over the earth] against their will. If, then, you do not help them, who will?'[1]

Bāyazīd, however, was an intensely religious man, a Muslim, and that means 'one who willingly submits' to God and his incomprehensible ways. Lucretius knew nothing of the one God whom the Hebrews substituted for the merry throng of immoral immortals that plagued the pagan world, but he would surely have found this one omnipotent tyrant of what monotheists are pleased to call 'true' religion far more oppressive than the many gods he knew and strenuously denied. For if there are lots of gods about the place there is a fair chance that they will be at odds with each other and it will be open to human beings to play them off against each other, but if there is *only* one omnipotent Lord whose behaviour seems to be utterly capricious, what chance have we? It was against this whole divine hocus-pocus that Lucretius, in the name of his master, Epicurus, revolted. The whole thing was a monstrous lie thought up by ignorant priests. To be religious is to be a slave, and not only to be a slave but to be the slave of monsters you have yourself thought up.

As usual, as Ecclesiastes said, there is nothing new under the

sun. The modern revolt against religion dating from the Enlightenment had all happened before in ancient Greece, which
put philosophy in the place of religion, and by 'philosophy' the
Greeks meant not only rational discourse but mathematics,
astronomy, physics, ethics, politics (which, of course, included
what are now called the 'social sciences') – the lot. There was
even room for theology if by that you mean the search for a
first cause by which all else can be rationally explained; but
there was no room for theology as currently understood by
Christians, that is, as far as I understand this supremely tedious
thing, the interpretation of what Christians are pleased to call
'Revelation' according to their own tortuous and frequently
silly ideas. The Greeks and their disciple Lucretius knew nothing
of divine 'revelation': they had only their traditional myths
which they, unlike their Jewish contemporaries, very soon came
to realise were more often than not both silly and amoral. To
deliver mankind from this minor tyranny Lucretius conceived
to be his bounden duty. The words with which he described the
task he had set himself have a curiously modern ring, if by
modern we mean the ideological climate that prevailed at the
beginning of this century – Comte, Marx, Freud and all the rest.
Perhaps if this is what we mean we should rename our world
not only the post-Christian world but the post-modern world;
for religion, having been escorted politely out of the front door,
has returned surreptitiously by the tradesman's entrance coyly
transformed into 'religious studies', the post-modern answer to
secularism. Or is it not rather the post-modern ally of secularism
of which Lucretius might have approved, since to teach about
religion is not to be religious, to teach about the irrational is
not (or ought not) to be irrational. Yes, Lucretius might
have approved, for what he says of religion could not by the
wildest stretch of the imagination apply to anything so anodyne
as 'religious studies'. This is what he says:

'When man's life lay for all to see foully grovelling upon the
ground, crushed beneath the weight of religion which displayed
her head from the regions of heaven, threatening mortals from
on high with her grisly glance, a man of Greece was the first
who dared raise mortal eyes against her, the first to make a
stand against her; for neither the prestige of the gods, nor

thunderbolts, nor the sky with its menacing roar could restrain him, but only goaded on the eager spirit of his soul the more, so that he, the first of all, should crave to smash the constricting bars of nature's gates. And so the living power of his soul won through, and forth he marched far beyond the flaming walls of the universe as he surveyed the immeasurable All in his mind and spirit. From there he brought back to us, in triumph, [the knowledge of] what can come into being and what can not, and how its finite potential and its proper end inhere sublimely in each thing in accordance with its nature. Hence religion is herself cast down in her turn and trampled underfoot while [his] victory has made *us* heaven's equals.[2]

This break-through is man's emancipation from all and any belief in the supernatural and the terrors it inspires. To the religious it is blasphemy, for it means that man deifies himself, thereby, as the Book of Genesis says, becoming 'like gods, knowing good and evil'.[3] For, though it may be true that God or the gods restrain man from evil, it is equally true that they are themselves beyond good and evil and hence, as Lucretius rightly points out 'all too often it is religion itself which has spawned criminal and impious deeds'.[4]

What kind of 'criminal and impious deeds' religion 'spawns' we know only too well from the history of Christian Europe – persecution of heretics, wars against the 'infidel', wars of one sort of Christian against another, and so on. But this kind of 'criminal and impious deeds' we inherit from the Jews, not from the Greeks. It is typical of the ancient Jewish religion, many of whose worst elements have seeped into our own culture: it is not typical of religion as such. What Lucretius had in mind was rather the cruelty of many ancient religious rites and, more important, the misery that man inflicted upon himself through his speculations on the nature of the 'other world' and his refusal to accept death as final and total extinction.

His anti-religious diatribe is triggered off by the first of these, in this case the practice of human sacrifice as exemplified by the sacrifice of Iphigenia in Aulis at the hands of her own father to the implacable goddess Artemis, who will not let the Greek armies proceed to Troy unless a spotless virgin is sacrificed to her. This particular act of barbarism drew those savagely anguished words which I have used for the title of this chapter from the lips of the rationalist Lucretius: 'So powerful has religion been to convince men to evil things.'

But, it may well be objected, human sacrifice, though it may have been wellnigh universal at a primitive stage of religion, has long since disappeared from the face of the earth. Very true, but it should not be forgotten that among the higher religions it is only Buddhism which has succeeded in dispensing with sacrifice altogether, and that the focal point of the Christian religion is precisely the Cross, the *locus* of what Christians consider to be the supreme sacrifice to end all lesser sacrifices in which a totally sinless man is done to death to propitiate his heavenly Father. What would Lucretius have made of that? I think this would have confirmed him in his belief that religion, insofar as it presupposes divine beings who delight in sacrifice, finds its natural and monstrous dénouement in the scandal and idiocy of the Cross as St Paul, never a man to mince his words, puts it.

But sacrifice, whether human or animal, is only one side of religion. As Lucretius saw and immediately went on to say, both the prestige of religion and its power to make human life on earth a misery lies in the fact that it claims to possess a privileged knowledge of what happens to us when we die. On this subject the different religions have very different ideas, but few of them are particularly encouraging.

The average Greek in Plato's time seems to have accepted death as no more than a snuffing out of life, and this does not seem to have worried him unduly any more than it did the Confucians and Taoists in China. 'When the soul leaves the body it no longer exists anywhere,' they thought, 'but on the day when a man dies, it is destroyed and snuffed out. The moment it is released from the body and leaves it behind, it is dispersed like breath or smoke, flies away and is no longer anything anywhere.'[5] Or, in the words of one of the more pessimistic sections of the Upanishads: 'After death there is no consciousness.'[6] If this is really so, and if, as most people would probably concede, there is at least nowadays a great deal more misery than happiness in life, what is all the fuss about? So, should you happen to be a Christian or Jew you might as well follow *this* equally wise *Biblical* counsel: 'So I commend enjoyment, since there is nothing good for a man to do here under the sun but to eat and drink and enjoy himself;

this is all that will remain with him to reward his toil throughout the span of life which God grants him here under the sun.'[7] Admirable advice, for, as the Confucians in China also taught, this is the only life we know: all else is speculation. So let us make the most of our TVs and offer our thanks to the scientists who made this earthly paradise possible.

Our non-existence after death the Old Testament Jews called Sheol: so 'whatever task lies to your hand, do it with all your might; because in Sheol, for which you are bound, there is neither doing nor thinking, neither understanding nor wisdom.'[8] This the Buddhists call Nirvāna, the later Buddhists and Taoists 'emptiness', Christians 'eternal rest'. But unfortunately none of them leave it at that: they will not leave us in peace. And we, apparently, do not want to be left in peace, for we shrink from non-existence and that terrible, gaping void. Try as we may to be rational animals, we rarely succeed since reason (and Aristotle and science) give us no ground to believe or hope that we will or can survive as individual persons. Hence, Lucretius regretfully says to the friend to whom his book is addressed:

> You yourself will some day or other try to make a clean break with me, falling a victim to the awesome pronouncements of soothsaying priests. Yes, even now they can think up for you many a dream [real enough] to upset the rational principles of life and shake all the happiness that may come your way with fear. And rightly so: for if men saw that the end of their tribulations was certain, they would be strong enough, at least to some degree, to stand up against the taboos of religion and the threats of priests. But now we have neither reason nor power to resist because we are bound to fear eternal punishments at death.[9]

Extinction is one thing, eternal punishment quite another. The first seemed wholly reasonable and desirable to the Epicurean Lucretius; the second was detestable from any point of view and all the more so because, in his opinion, it was no more than an inheritance derived from ignorant men who had believed themselves to be inspired by higher powers whose whims were law and who showed no love for men who, according even to Plato, were their chattels, to be treated with as much consideration as man himself shows to the other beasts, that is none at all.

These amiable ideas the Greeks derived from Mesopotamia which is pre-eminent among all the ancient civilisations for its low opinion of the gods as moral beings and for its excessively gloomy picture of the afterlife; and it is this depressing view of 'religion' that has been passed on to us both by the Greeks (with the schizophrenic Plato well to the fore) but also, and far more effectively, by the Jews.

Greek religion was of course polytheistic, and there is this at least to be said for polytheism: there is safety in numbers. If Athena lets you down, you can always turn to Apollo, whereas in Homer at least even Zeus, the acknowledged head of the pantheon, can be and is outwitted by his cow-eyed wife, Hera, who seems to have an uncanny knack of picking the winning side. In other words, she knows that even almighty Zeus cannot alter what has already been decreed by an ineluctable destiny; and so, with a ruthless consistency, she conforms her own inflexible will to what must in the long run come to pass. She is patient, and hers usually turns out to be the winning side. For, like all the gods, she has her favourites, and favouritism is the main characteristic of gods in general. However, the evils of religion were at least partially overcome in elitist circles by the rise of philosophy in the broadest sense of that word. But it was not Lucretius' hero Epicurus who first put paid to the ancient superstitions and the newer ones which invaded Greece from the barbarous north and east but Aristotle who, following the insights of his predecessors, sought and thought he had found one single eternal principle in and through which the universe could be explained. With Aristotle reason emerges as the ultimate arbiter in the affairs of men – reason, that is, supplemented in due measure by intuitive insight into those realms of human life which, because they are beyond space and time and causation, are necessarily inaccessible to discursive thought. These realms are the proper sphere of religion. That they do in fact exist is proved, the mystics say (as does Aristotle), by the fact that they have themselves experienced them. But, since they add that human speech is quite inadequate to describe them, their ecstasies leave most of us unmoved. Some allege that they are the supreme good; others – dangerously – aver that they are beyond good and evil; but, when pressed, both mystics and non-mystics would agree that, from the point of view of living out our lives on earth, they are utterly irrelevant.

In Greece, then, the undisciplined throng of quarrelsome gods was superseded by a metaphysical Absolute which was so remote as to be quite harmless: unlike the God or gods of religion it did not persuade men to evil deeds. In Israel, however, things were very different. Gradually the Jewish national God, Yahweh, ousted all the other gods and asserted himself as the One God, True and Holy. This assertion of the absolute unity and supremacy of God has generally been regarded as being the unique and uniquely valuable contribution of the Jewish race to mankind. In fact it raises far more problems than it solves. If the gods were both immoral and frivolous, then they could always be played off against each other, but if there is only one God who boasts of having created good and evil,[10] and glories in the destruction he wreaks, then what chance has man but to bow to the will of the divine Monster? And so it is that the evils attributed to the pagan gods and their ignorant devotees are as nothing compared with the evils attributed by the Jews to the Lord God of Israel. The Greek gods never commanded genocide as the Lord God commanded it to Joshua in the case of Jericho[11] and to Saul in the case of the Amalekites.[12] The latter case is so shocking, so wicked, that it deserves to be quoted in full in case any who may be Jew or Christian should have forgotten it and in order that those who have not been schooled in the 'Good' Book may obtain some inkling of just how 'good' it is. The prophet Samuel is speaking to Saul:

'This is the very word of the Lord of Hosts [meaning 'armies']: "I am resolved to punish the Amalekites and destroy them, and put their property under a ban. Spare no one: put them all to death, men and women, children and babes in arms, herds and flocks, camels and asses.'

Because Saul showed some humanity and did not fulfil Yahweh's diabolic command to the full, he was rejected 'because the Lord had repented of having made him king of Israel'.[13] And as if that were not enough, the wretched man was driven mad, or, in the 'religious' language of the Bible, 'an evil spirit from God seized upon Saul; he fell into a frenzy'.[14] What a God! First he orders genocide; secondly, he punishes the wretched Saul for showing even the faintest trace of human feeling; thirdly, he, the allegedly changeless one, changes his mind and 'repents'; fourthly, he whom we are extolled to acknowledge as 'good' sends an evil spirit *from himself* to drive Saul mad. What 'evil' has the religion of the Greeks to offer comparable to this? No, the 'higher' religion the discovery of which is held to reflect eternal credit on the Jews was far worse than anything Lucretius had condemned. It is an evil thing for a family to be in a semi-permanent state of civil war as were the Greek gods; it is far more evil for an individual to be at war with himself, and that is precisely and exactly the state of mind of the Lord God of Israel who rants and raves throughout the Old Testament, lurching from paroxysms of rage into equally disquieting paroxysms of passionate love.

As to Christianity and all that mealy-mouthed claptrap about 'Gentle Jesus meek and mild', perhaps it is not beside the point to remind the reader that this same Jesus is quoted as saying: 'You must not think that I have come to bring peace to the earth; I have not come to bring peace, but a sword. I have come to set a man against his father, a daughter against her mother, a son's wife against her mother-in-law; and a man will find his enemies under his own roof.'[15] Strange words one may think, to proceed from the mouth of the 'Prince of Peace'. Yet not so strange since there is no religion without paradox, and no Semitic religion without violent paradox. Theology tries to smooth over these all too rough edges of religion, but theology is little more than a pathetic effort of human reason fettered by irrational faith to reconcile the divine inconsistencies with something that has the specious appearance of rationality. Even so the twin results of all this laborious ratiocination are nevertheless admitted by all to be incomprehensible 'mysteries' – the Incarnation and the Trinity, both 'impossible' and 'absurd', as Tertullian rightly observed, but nonetheless absurdities for which men were prepared to face persecution and death. Let us change Lucretius' dictum here and say: 'So powerful has religion been to convince men of lunatic things!'

The evils of Islam are as evident as those of its parent religion, Judaism, but since they have been the object of constant Christian polemic we need not expatiate on them here. We need say little of the Islamic doctrine of the torments of hell since all religions including Buddhism revel in these, but some of us may boggle at the Islamic 'revelation' that many were actually *created* for hell, and that God himself leads astray whom he will: 'whomsoever God guides, he is rightly guided; and whom he leads astray, they are the losers. *We have created for hell many jinn and men.*'[16] And 'assuredly I shall fill hell with jinn and men together'.[17] Hell on its side is only too happy to play its full part in this diabolically divine comedy, for God says to Hell, 'Are you full up?' to which Hell cheerfully replies, 'Haven't you yet more?'[18] And of course there can be no question of your being saved by any good deeds you may have done since your salvation or damnation has been settled once and for all from the beginning of the world. As for Luther salvation is by faith alone, and faith is a grace gratuitously bestowed by God; and grace of course means favouritism, and favouritism is rarely considered as being consistent with justice. But the divine 'justice', we are told, like all things divine, in no way resembles human justice. It cannot indeed possibly do so since this God, as he reveals himself in the Old and New Testaments and in the Koran, is neither just nor good as we understand justice and goodness. As the Zoroastrians never tire of pointing out, he is both God and the Devil all rolled into one. So much for the Semitic God.

Now let us briefly consider the Indians. What 'evil' have *they* thought up for us? The dominant phobia in the West nowadays seems to be the fear of death. Though few believe in an afterlife any more, and though it can scarcely be said that the afterlife as depicted in the Semitic religions has any attractions except for the believer (and it must be noted in passing that orthodox Muslims, Jews and Christians each believe that they have an exclusive claim to the Kingdom of Heaven), nevertheless modern man, against all reason, is terrified of being snuffed out. For the Indians the exact opposite is true: the final horror is not the certainty of absolute death but the certainty of unending life, and, according to the mainstream of Indian religion, life, because it is transient, is therefore constant anxiety, pain, and unease. The wheel of existence rolls relentlessly on and with each turning of the wheel you become more deeply involved in this senseless merry-go-round from which there is no escape. At the very centre of all Indian religion, whether Hindu, Buddhist or Jain, stands the dogma of reincarnation (Indians would call it the *fact* of reincarnation) and, given the fact that the climate of India is about as unpleasant as it can be and that the majority of the population haven't enough to eat, the prospect of being born, growing old, and dying for untold aeons is almost too grievous to be borne. Thus Hinduism is afflicted by a triple evil – an Absolute who cares nothing for the world, a host of gods quite as capricious as their Greek counterparts, and the curse of reincarnation. Admittedly 'the gods' later tend to coalesce into one God who is identical with the Absolute in essence but not identical with it insofar as he, like the Jewish Yahweh, concerns himself with men in our world of time and space. Like Yahweh, too, he is totally unpredictable and much given to favouritism, otherwise called grace. It was the Buddha's great achievement that he abolished the Absolute and with it God, though retaining the gods as picturesque cosmic furniture, thereby reducing religion to a stark confrontation of man with the relentless process of coming-to-be and passing away of which reincarnation formed an indispensable part. In order to make it applicable to Buddhism we would have to change Lucretius' dictum to this: 'So powerful has religion been to convince man that *the world* is evil.'

The absence of a vengeful God does indeed lend Buddhism a certain attraction since Buddhist morality derives not from the commands and prohibitions of an inscrutable and unpredictable God but from an enlightened self-interest which paradoxically arises from a refusal to admit that there is any such thing as an individual self. To realise this is to realise 'death without rebirth', a situation which the average Greek of Plato's time accepted as a matter of course without making too much fuss about it. Buddhism, however, was not content to take the good and the bad in life in its stride nor could it accept death as final. Inheriting the belief that rebirth follows on death as inevitably as death does on birth, it sought (and found) a condition which transcended the whole cyclical process and which in its timeless peace (the Christian 'eternal rest') could be accurately described as eternal death. And so the Zen Buddhists at last hit upon the cheerful formula: 'Die while yet alive, and be completely dead.' In the West Plato and the Stoics said much the same thing, but the hero of this chapter, Lucretius, was neither a Platonist nor a Stoic. He was an Epicurean, opposed alike to the wickedness of the religion of gods and God and to renunciation of this world as being of its very nature evil. Thus, while it would be absurd to deny that 'religion' has at times been responsible for much good, it would be no less absurd to deny that it has been a powerful force 'to convince men of evil things' that may or may not exist but whose presumed existence only adds to the immense burden of evil that weighs upon us in our everyday lives. Perhaps, after all, we are better off without it.

Chapter 5

The Scandal of Christ

child / simple / innocent

Christians on the whole are very ordinary people. That this should be so is itself extraordinary, for of all the world religions Christianity is by far the most extraordinary – 'impossible' and 'absurd' as Tertullian said without any exaggeration at all, a 'scandal' to the Jews and sheer 'feeble-mindedness' (*mōron*) to the Greeks.[1] *Mōron*, it may be said, translated in most English versions as 'folly' or 'foolishness', is a quality applied to children (in modern Greek a *mōron paidhi* means simply a very small child) and, at least by Euripides,[2] to women, regarded by the Greeks as a pretty scatterbrained lot. Yet St Paul is bold enough to apply the term to God himself – a childish, womanish, feebleminded God then, which surely should give us pause to think. *pollyanna*

Reared in Christianity as most of us have been, we tend to take it as the religious norm from the standpoint of which other religions must be seen if not judged. In this we are wrong. Christianity is not the norm of anything but a monstrous abnormality: it does not fit into the pattern of the other world religions at all. We are surely wrong in seeing ourselves as the legitimate heirs to the Jewish dispensation of the Old Covenant. We are not. If anything we are a monstrous brood of bastards, and that is more or less how orthodox Jewry sees us. For these Jews Christianity is anything but a natural development out of Judaism: it is a violent and wholly illegitimate distortion of it. The 'prophecies' with which the writers of the New Testament (and particularly St Matthew) seek to bolster up the gospel story and the Pauline claims on behalf of Jesus are seen to be torn violently out of context and used in a sense that had never occurred to any traditional Jew in the wildest flights of his imagination. Scandal it certainly is, for it is not nice for the race that regarded itself as being the uniquely chosen people of God to be told by an apparently mad rabbi that it has been rejected by

Nazareth upriser

that very God who chose it because it failed to see in him not only the Messiah, the 'Lord's anointed' and predestined deliverer of Israel from alien rule, but also the 'Son of God', a concept that can only be repugnant to any self-respecting monotheist. Jesus is indeed a scandal – a stumbling-block – and the Jews have stumbled over him ever since; in faithfulness to their own election and tradition, which forbade them to have any gods but Yahweh,[3] they have not bowed down and worshipped what they hold to be a human idol. That they should not have done so is the most natural thing in the world, for to have done so would have meant a complete reversal of all they held most sacred – the complete Oneness and Sovereignty of God, the triumph of the long-awaited Messiah, and the absolute validity of God's Law. Given their premises, their rejection of Jesus was wholly rational while the claims made either by Jesus or others on his behalf were not only blasphemous but wholly irrational. They may have been mistaken in over-rationalising their religion, since religion itself is not a rational pursuit but man's response to the irrationality of his own condition. It is rather the task of theology to rationalise the irrational, and that is why it never succeeds.

So much for the Jewish view of Christianity. Let us now consider it from the more general point of view of the world religions as a whole.

No student of religion at however elementary a stage can fail to be impressed by the obvious fact that there is a gulf fixed between the religions associated with Judaism on the one hand and those deriving from or associated with India on the other. They do not seem to be dealing with the same subject-matter. On the one side you have prophetic religion, on the other mystical. Perhaps the two complement each other: if you over-emphasize the one, then the other will tend to come back by the back door, and before you know where you are it will have taken possession of the servants' quarters and the gentry will be faced with the awkward problem of how to deal with an irruption of what appears to be collective insanity among the staff. That this is so might explain the present vogue of Eastern mysticism that has gripped so many of the young and not so young today. This has taken the Christian religious establishment by surprise, and it is worrying because conventional Christians simply do not

understand what these strange enthusiasts and their gurus are
talking about. They don't seem to be interested in God at all
but in transcendental states of consciousness which they describe
as Nirvāna, *Satori*, 'emptiness', the Void, Brahman, 'suchness',
and the like. This is all very confusing. Let us then consider the
essential difference between these two types of religion – the
prophetic and the mystical.

Prophetic religion is deeply concerned with what goes on in this
world: the prophet is a man with a message to men on how they
should behave in general or to particular men on what they
should do in given concrete circumstances. For Christians
prophecy is associated above all with Israel, the chosen race, for,
according to their extraordinary way of thinking, the Hebrew
prophets all pointed towards the coming of Jesus, the Word of
God made flesh, who, since he was God himself appearing in
human form, had necessarily brought prophecy to an end. Jewish
prophecy, however, is only one branch of prophecy in general,
though it has its special characteristics as we shall see. In Greece
and Rome too the divine powers made their will known through
prophets or prophetesses who were often associated with a
particular holy place, as in the case of the Pythian oracle at Delphi.
Their prophecies, however, were usually cryptic and needed to be
interpreted by experts (the case of Apollo's clear command to
Orestes to murder his mother seems to be exceptional). The
case of the Hebrew prophets, however, was quite different. True
'schools' of prophets in the Greek sense of the word did exist
in Israel,[4] but they were very different from the great prophets
of the Old Testament. They were very much more like the
Dionysian enthusiasts in Greece whose 'ecstasies' (getting outside
oneself, that is) could lead to deplorable results, or the dancing
dervishes of a later age who could be *used* for political purposes
but whose ecstatic utterances rarely had any reference to current
affairs. The 'authentic' prophets of Israel were quite different
from this since they spoke in the name not of the maniac God
Dionysius but in the name of the 'Lord God of Israel', a uniquely
'jealous' God who claimed absolute obedience to his Law and the
spirit of his Law which, however eccentric his own actions might
appear to men, was nonetheless a Law which, at least as interpreted
by the prophets, demanded of man justice and mercy above all
things. The prophets were, then, always a thorn in the flesh of

the powers that be: like the God they claimed to represent they were severe to the point of vindictiveness. As the editors of the Jerusalem Bible put it: 'There are two aspects to the message, threat and consolation. Jeremiah was sent "to tear up and to knock down, to build up and to plant." And indeed the message often makes bitter hearing, a tissue of menaces and reproaches, so much so that severity comes to be a sign that a prophet is genuine.'[5] But, as with Cassandra in Greece, a 'true' prophetess, the warnings are never heeded or, if heeded, it is already too late. Prophecy, then, is an urgent message delivered to men (in this case Jewish men) at critical points in their history in time. It is 'the God of Abraham, the God of Isaac, the God of Jacob' who speaks, 'not the God of the philosophers and scientists,' as Pascal said.

But does this God only speak to the Jews? On the face of it, and if we are not prepared to write God off as totally irrational, 'childish', and 'silly', this would seem improbable. And in fact two prophets do appear outside Israel whose credentials seem every bit as valid as those of the Prophets of the Old Testament. These are Zoroaster, who lived in eastern Iran traditionally some six hundred years before Christ, and, far more important, Muhammad, the Prophet of Arabia, who lived six hundred years after him.

For Christians Zoroaster and Zoroastrianism present little difficulty. It is well known that early Judaism was so this-worldly that it paid little attention to the afterlife. If this existed at all it was a pretty miserable state of existence called Sheol in the Old Testament. In this grim 'pit' from which there is no return the dead can scarcely be said to exist at all since they know nothing, remember nothing, receive no reward,[6] are forgotten by God[7] to whom they no longer have any access. There was as yet no idea of a personal afterlife in which good deeds were rewarded and evil ones punished. These ideas only entered Judaism after the Babylonian captivity and the liberation of the Jews by Cyrus, the Persian, whom Isaiah describes as the Lord's anointed, that is, in Hebrew, the Lord's 'Messiah'.

That the Jews should be open to Persian religious ideas need not surprise us since the Persians were their liberators and some at least of them were monotheists. The disciples of Zoroaster were such, except that their monotheism was modified by the existence of the Devil, whose status was at first left vague but who later was raised to the rank of an eternal principle utterly opposed to the good and fruitful God and all his ways; he is the power of death and destruction, a murderer, a liar and a deceiver. Such a monstrous independent power exists nowhere in the Old Testament, but he begins to appear in the inter-testamentary writings and is menacingly present in the New, particularly in the writings attributed to John. This idea, as well as the existence of heaven and hell and the rewards and punishments that go with them, the Jews and through them the Christians almost certainly owed to the Zoroastrians, and since they are the doctrines attributed to Zoroaster personally it would seem that even the most orthodox Christian would have little difficulty in accepting Zoroaster as being a genuine prophet outside Israel, a prophet inspired by the same one God to 'enlighten the gentiles', as the Hebrew prophets had been inspired to 'fill out' the Law of Moses. Zoroaster is a stumbling-block to no one, not even to the Muslims who took on his leading ideas – not directly but through their Jewish and Christian predecessors – and were thus prevailed upon, though with some reluctance on their part, to accept them as 'people of the Book', that is to say as being in receipt of a genuinely divine revelation.

But what of Muhammad and the revelation of which he claimed to be the mouthpiece? For Christians he is indeed a stumbling-block which they cannot surmount: they can only sidle round it and this is what they have consistently done. Yet it is Muhammad who stands squarely within the basically Jewish tradition of strict monotheism, not Jesus, whom the Christians made equal to God thereby irreparably impairing his absolute oneness. The vast majority of the Jews had rejected Jesus of Nazareth and the claims to divinity made either by him or on his behalf as being a monstrous perversion of the whole Jewish concept of God, even an outright denial of it. The Muslims did not do this. Indeed, what is so pathetic in the whole history of Christian-Muslim relations is that the Koran, which Muslims claim is the divine Word made *Book*, consistently vindicates the man Jesus against the calumnies levelled against him and his mother by the Jews. It was perfectly clear to Muhammad that something very strange had happened among the 'people of the Book' by which he meant primarily the Jews and Christians. We know next to nothing about his early career but it is clear that in his formative years he must have had contact with both Jews and Christians and that he considered both to be the recipients of a revelation from the One True God, but it very soon became clear to him that they not only disagreed but were violently at odds with each other on the question of the status of Jesus the Messiah, as Muhammad himself calls him. Was he a prophet? Was he the 'Word' of God, or the 'Son' of God? Was he a 'spirit' from God? Was he a wonder worker? Was his mother a virgin, as the Christians claimed, or was she a whore, as the Jews more than implied? What was he, and who was to decide? Obviously not the Jews, whose hatred of the Christians who had broken away from them had so blinded them that they could not see that Jesus was in the line of the true prophets and that the authenticity of his mission had been proved by his miracles, by the fact that he raised others from the dead 'with God's permission',[8] and that he himself had been taken up to heaven without having to suffer death.[9] If, however, the Jews were biased, the same was true of the Christians; for they made claims on behalf of Jesus that were monstrously at variance with the pure monotheistic faith and which Jesus himself would have repudiated with horror. Hence only God can choose between them[10] and this he does through the final revelation of his Word made *Book* in the shape of the Koran which must necessarily contain all truth.

All this seems perfectly logical. If God reveals himself through Prophets, and principally through Moses and Jesus, the prophets of the Jews and Christians respectively, and if these two sects are violently at loggerheads with each other on the subject of Jesus, then it must follow that one or other of the parties to the dispute or both of them must have falsified the scripture entrusted to them, and that the matter can only be settled by a final revelation which took shape as the Koran, which is not only the Word made Book but also the *ipsissima verba* of God inscribed for all eternity in what the Koran calls the 'Preserved Tablet'. Since the Koran accepts almost all the claims that the Christians make on behalf of Jesus, including their claim that he is the 'Word of Truth'[11] or at least 'His Word which he cast upon Mary',[12] and since it repeatedly denounces the Jews for having broken the covenant which was entrusted to them,[13] it is scarcely surprising that the Muslims were genuinely and bitterly disappointed at the Christian establishment's refusal to accept the new dispensation since they continued obstinately to adhere to the two 'polytheistic' doctrines they had introduced and which, according to the Koran, Jesus had himself rejected with horror – the Incarnation and the Trinity. There might be bitter enmity between Muslim and Jew on many scores, but on the subject of the absolute unity of God they were in full agreement. It is impious to speak of God having a Son, and both impious and absurd to speak of God becoming a man and asserting of God that he is not only One but Three.

Islam, then, sees itself as God's final and unadulterated revelation to man, perfecting all past revelations with which it is essentially identical and correcting the human errors introduced by the unworthy followers of Moses and Jesus respectively. This Muslim claim seems to me very strong, and it explains why Christians have never succeeded in converting Muslims in any significant numbers except by force. To a Muslim it makes about as much sense to become a Christian as it makes to the Christian to become a Jew. It is a step *back* to an older and imperfect dispensation which the new and perfect one has superseded. So much, then, must suffice for the prophetic tradition of which Christianity is the middle term, not the end.

How do matters stand with the mystical religions of India, and how does Christianity appear to them?

Before discussing this we must consider what the premises from which they start are and how, if at all, the 'mysteries' of the Incarnation and the Trinity can be fitted into them. Now it is well known that the one dogma which holds the three ancient religions of India – Hinduism, Buddhism, and Jainism – together is that of reincarnation, which is itself only one aspect of the more general theory of *samsāra*, the belief based on observed fact that the world as we know it is in a permanent state of flux; but the flux itself is not a random affair but governed by an inexorable law of cause and effect, what is usually called the law of *Karma*, the law of 'action', and the 'fruits' that each and every action is bound to bear. As applied to man this law is essentially a moral law, however differently morality may be interpreted in the three religions. But morality in itself is not enough since whatever you do, be it evil or good, must necessarily bind you to the wheel of existence from which there would appear to be no escape. India's answer to Job, then, is simple and has a certain logic which seems to make sense of the problem of evil. In the Old Testament Job's anguish at the apparent injustice of God which allowed the wicked to prosper and the righteous to suffer met with no response from his inexorable tormentor except the display of naked power, since the Zoroastrian notion of rewards and punishments being meted out to the good and the wicked respectively in future states called heaven and hell had not yet percolated into the mainstream of Jewish thought. In India, however, the theory of reincarnation, which came to be regarded more and more as a *fact* and not simply a dogma, seemed to explain everything. If you did not pay for the evil you had done in this life, you would pay for it in a future one, and in like manner the good would receive their appropriate reward. But even the joys of the many heavens which an Indian mind thought up provided no solution, for they too must come to an end. In this world life and death are simply the twin facets of the same process. As the Bhagavad Gītā (2.27) says: 'For sure is the death of all that is born, sure is the birth of all that dies: so in a matter that no one can prevent you have no cause to grieve.' The round of birth and death is endless – and endlessly wearisome. 'Salvation', then, can only mean a final end to the whole dreary process which will release you into a state where there is neither birth nor death and therefore no life which, as usually conceived of, is the intermediary state between the two. To speak of 'eternal life', then, as Christians normally do, so far from being 'good news' is an almost obscene 'scandal', totally unacceptable and, if not exactly childish, then, from the higher standpoint of 'pure' spirituality, rather vulgar. To speak of 'eternal *rest*' makes Indian sense; to speak of eternal *life*, too, makes sense but in a very different way. Indeed it is received as an almost axiomatic truth, but it is a truth that all enlightened men found abhorrent and which they sought to transcend. The Christian doctrine of the resurrection of the body, however 'spiritual' that body might be, must then appear as a grave scandal to the Indians. So far from being 'good news', it is not news at all: it is a well-known and most deplorable fact. True, cases are recorded in which exceptionally holy men are said to have ascended into heaven while still in the body as Jesus is said to have done in the Muslim tradition. Most notable among these was Yudhishthira,

the ascetically saintly and pacifist hero of the *Mahābhārata,*
India's enormous epic, but the first thing he did on arriving there
was to curse the gods for rewarding what *he* considered to be
injustice; and even after he had been suitably mollified by being
bathed in the heavenly Ganges, he was given to understand that
he would have to be incarnated on earth once more before he
could achieve his final release from temporal life, his 'eternal
rest' in which there is neither coming-to-be nor passing away,
neither birth nor death nor the life that runs its course between
the two. To ascend into heaven is not enough, for you must
transcend heaven with its joys, both vulgar and refined, before
you can achieve that 'peace which passes all understanding' of
which Paul speaks.

With the exception of Origen and some other eccentrics,
Christians have not taken to the doctrine of reincarnation
whereas the Muslims abominate the whole idea. On the question
of the concept of the Incarnation of God as man, the Indians
are divided – and necessarily so, since if there is no God, no
supreme Being as opposed to the prolific throng of polytheistic
deities, then plainly there can be no incarnation that remotely
corresponds to what Christians mean by that term. Since neither
the Buddhists nor the Jains accept a God in the Semitic sense
of that word, that is the Creator, Sustainer, and absolute Ruler
of the universe, we can scarcely speak of an incarnation of 'God'
as we understand him. Whether we can usefully make use of the
term in some other sense we shall see later.

In Hinduism, however, things are very different. By the time
the Upanishads were written (*c*. 800–300 BC) the ancient pantheon
had not indeed ceased to exist but had lost all its old importance.
The gods no longer mattered, but what *did* matter was the
supreme impersonal Absolute which was both the true Self of
the universe and the true Self of every individual man. To
realise this identity meant to realise oneself as the Eternal, that
is the changeless one which alone truly *is*, or as pure consciousness,
as one of the Upanishads puts it.[14] This may be ontologically
true but, if so, it is very far indeed from obvious to us phenomenal
creatures, humanly conditioned as we are. To realise this you need
the guidance of a guru, a spiritual guide whether he be human
or divine. For this to be at all possible it would be necessary
for the impersonal Absolute to become personalised as a God;

and this is in fact what took place. The Absolute was, then, personalised in the form of two quite insignificant ancient gods (how and why these two were chosen is still far from clear), Shiva and Vishnu. Shiva, the more awe-inspiring of the two, was, in this temporal world of ours, manifested as dwelling high up in the Himalayas, though manifesting himself in myth and legend in alarmingly diverse ways; he did not become incarnate in human form. His rival, Vishnu (with whom he was, from the absolute point of view, identical), did manifest himself not only in human form but also in a variety of animal forms such as a fish or a boar. The reason for his successive incarnations he himself explains in his own particular scripture, the Bhagavad Gītā (4.7–8): 'For', he says, 'whenever the law of righteousness withers away and lawlessness arises, then do I generate myself [on earth]. For the protection of the good, for the destruction of evil-doers, for the setting up of the law of righteousness I come into being age after age.'

This seems reasonable enough, and it makes room for the incarnation of God (Vishnu) as Jesus Christ too. The average Hindu has no difficulty in accepting this but has the greatest difficulty in understanding why the Christians on their side should be so unwilling to admit God's incarnations at least as Krishna and Rāma as being as genuine as his incarnation as Jesus. The fact that both Rāma and Krishna are legendary characters makes no difference at all to them since the 'God of history' leaves them quite cold, and they are not slow to point out that the present vogue for 'demythologisation' proves that modern Christians no longer attach much importance to the historical Jesus. As to the 'Christ-event', they may be forgiven for failing to understand what this particular neologism is supposed to mean. In any case, why should they accept a once-and-for-all incarnation which is supposed to have brought salvation to mankind when mankind has quite obviously not been saved? If anything, since the occurrence of the 'Christ-event' it is at least arguable that things have got considerably worse. Salvation, then, must be a matter of perpetual renewal, of successive incarnations among which, incidentally, they somewhat incongruously include the Buddha – and are quite prepared to accept not only Jesus but Muhammad too, not to mention such charismatic figures as Caitanya in the sixteenth century, Rāmakrishna in the nineteenth, and Mahātma Gandhi and Sri Aurobindo in the twentieth. God, they feel, does not leave the world without witness. As to Christ's sacrificial death on the Cross, they understand this as little as the Jews or Muslims or, indeed, as the majority of Christians themselves do. For how on earth is the agony of one man for three hours on a cross supposed to atone for the sins of the world, even if that man is God incarnate? Such a barbaric return to the principle of redemptive human sacrifice cannot be expected to appeal to any rational mind. The Cross is at most incidental: what is essential and what they can readily understand is that the divine Logos 'was inserted into mankind' (*enēnthrōpēsen*) so that we might be deified, (*theopoiēthōmen*, 'made god(s)'), as Athanasius puts it.[15] To the orthodox Jew or Muslim this would be scandalous blasphemy; but to the Hindu it is perhaps an understatement, for in our inmost essence we already *are* 'gods' though we do not know it. We are 'gods' in the sense that we are *essentially* independent of time and space and the world that is conditioned by them, and only *accidentally* associated with them and fettered by them. In this context the 'Christ-event' like the 'Krishna-event' makes sense: God, the timelessly eternal, is incarnated in human form, declares to man the way of salvation by which he may attain freedom from this world and above all from his self-assertive and acquisitive ego, dies, and, by dying to the world, regains his divine and timeless status. For the Hindus there is nothing scandalous in this, but there is folly and childishness in thinking this can happen only once, for according to them it is happening every day.

How do matters stand with the Buddhists? As we have seen, to speak of the incarnation of God in a Christian sense cannot mean anything since there is no God in the Christian sense. But what is the nature of the Buddha himself? Clearly, even according to the earliest accounts, he is no ordinary mortal at least after he has attained enlightenment. Apart from the supernatural powers attributed to him his pre-eminence is displayed by the fact that he is 'teacher of *gods* and men' – and the gods include Brahmā, the greatest of them all, who *thinks* he is the first cause and creator of the universe but is in fact nothing of the sort.[16] He is, then, the manifestation in time of a being who has descended from a totally different form of existence to which even the greatest of the gods, Brahmā, has no access. He is, indeed, the *of good, love + peace.*

timeless Truth incarnated in the form of Gotama, later called the 'Buddha', the one who is fully 'awake' because he has seen *through* the transient nature of the word *into* what is permanent and lies byond it and which is, in fact, his own true nature. In this respect one might well say that he is eternal Truth 'inserted into mankind'. Like the Hindu Vishnu he reappears time and again and for the same purpose; for the words of the Bhagavad Gītā are applicable to him too: 'For the setting up of the law of righteousness I come into being age after age.' And the 'law of righteousness' he brings is in essence the same law of self-giving and self-denial preached by Jesus in the Sermon on the Mount. But the Christian interpretation of the message of the 'Word' or 'Truth' made flesh remains if not a scandal then at least 'childishness' to the Buddhists, for what is of its nature transient must be fraught with anxiety and unease – with suffering, if you like. And this cannot be transformed into its opposite: it can only be shown to be in some sense unreal. It can be transcended but not transmuted. Salvation, then, consists in being saved *from* it since *it* – this world of space and time – you cannot save. To try to do so is Christian 'childishness' – ineptitude, for it means not being fully 'awake' to the gulf that separates this world from the timeless and eternal. The Buddhists of the earlier dispensation would almost certainly have condemned this mad idea of saving the world as one of the fruits of *avijjā*, that cosmic 'ignorance' which mistakes the unreal for the real and which is the root sin of mankind.

From the point of view of the other world religions, then, it can be said that Christianity alone among them *is* a scandal and sheer lunacy: a scandal – an insurmountable stumbling-block – to the uncompromising prophetic monotheism of both Judaism and Islam, and lunacy, childishness, feeblemindedness (call it what you will) to the weary wisdom of the Indian and Indianised East.

Chapter 6

Why not Islam?

The interest in non-Christian religions in the United States and in England has taken two forms, the one popular, the other academic. The first of these has turned almost exclusively to Hindu and Buddhist mysticism and can be seen as an energetic reaction against the dogmatic and until very recently rigid structure of institutionalised Christianity and a search for a lived *experience* of the freedom of the spirit which is held to be the true content of mysticism, obscured in Christianity by the basic dogma of a transcendent God, the 'wholly Other' of Rudolf Otto and his numerous followers, but wholly untrammelled by any such concept in the higher reaches of Vedanta and Buddhism, particularly in its Zen manifestation. On the academic side the picture is less clear. There is, of course, the claim that the study of religion, like any other academic study, must be subjected to and controlled by the same principles of 'scientific' objectivity to which the other 'arts' subjects have been subjected, to their own undoing. But even here there would seem to be a bias in favour of the religions of India and the Far East as against Islam, largely, one supposes, in response to popular demand. The young are not interested in switching from one dogmatic monotheistic faith to another: hence they are little interested in Islam except when Islam itself is turned upside down and becomes Sūfism, which in its developed form is barely distinguishable from Vedanta. Indeed that egregious populariser Idries Shah has gone as far as to claim Zen as a manifestation of Sūfism, a proposition which from the historical point of view is nonsense and from the supposedly objective point of view of the strict academic detestable, since it is not telling the factual truth. However 'good' the intention may be the result will be evil, for in almost all religions not saturated with an amoral (call it 'transmoral' if you like) mysticism 'truth' and the 'good' are indissolubly united, for 'sooner or later', as Aristotle[1] rightly maintains, 'false "goods" must necessarily result in true evil'. Unfortunately, teachers of religious studies, being human and therefore not omniscient, are forced, in the very nature of the case, to rely on experts, real or allegedly so; and since it is the practice of publishers to advertise their authors as 'acknowledged experts' (acknowledged by whom?), they may well find that, since they are not competent to form an independent judgement on the evidence supplied by the 'experts', they are in fact perpetuating 'true evil' in the form of misunderstood or invented 'facts'. All this is as true of popular accounts of Sūfism as it is of Vedanta and Zen. And it is true not only of the more shameless popularisers but also of the most prestigious experts themselves. Even Massignon and Nicholson can err.

From all this it follows that, surrounded by so many pitfalls, the teacher of religious studies (like any teacher) must not only be learned, he must also possess academic humility to a rare degree. In order to teach you must first learn, and there is no end to the process of learning. But it is not enough to learn, you must also try to understand; and this is what Wilfrid Cantwell Smith was trying to point out in his essay 'Is the Qur'an the Word of God?'[2]

This essay, which Professor Cantwell Smith considered to be extremely 'radical' at the time, is now, in these days of the wider ecumenism and holy 'dialogue', taken for granted, which perhaps means no more than that lip-service to it has become *de rigueur*. Scholarship plus empathy is the recipe, or in Professor Cantwell Smith's more precise words: 'How the Qur'an came to be what it is, is one question, to which the Western sceptic has addressed himself. How the Qur'an came to do what it has done, for believing Muslims across the centuries since, is another: the actual life-giving source of the religious life of the continuing community.'[3]

This approach to Islam has been consistently pursued by Bishop Kenneth Cragg in a whole series of books inspired by a passionate desire to understand Islam and an almost tormented empathy which never seems quite to grasp why the Koran is to Muslims what it is. And the real reason why he never makes the final breakthrough is that, as a devout and wholly dedicated Christian, he has not seriously asked himself Cantwell Smith's question: 'Is the Qur'an the Word of God?' The reason is obvious, though it is rarely rammed down Christian throats with sufficient vigour, yet it is the only question that really matters and even the 'radical' Professor Cantwell Smith only poses the dreadful dilemma in a footnote.[4] In the rest of his essay it is ignored. However, he *has* stated it and encouraged us to bear it in mind when reading through his essay. This, then, is what he says:

> Christians are in danger of missing the full force of the Muslim position on this matter, by supposing that the analogy with the Qur'an is the Bible. Rather, the parallel is to the doctrine that Jesus Christ is the Word of God. Throughout this present discussion, this point should be borne vividly in mind: that the Muslim attitude to the Qur'an is the Christian attitude to Christ.

Unfortunately, Cantwell Smith, having made his point in this pregnant footnote, thereby ensuring that the cursory reader will skip it, makes no attempt to draw the consequences from the bitter dilemma it poses. If the Christian (and the agnostic) is to be confronted with the question of 'Is the Qur'an the Word of God?', then the Muslim too (and the agnostic) must be confronted with the rival question: 'Is Jesus Christ the Word of God?' Or, to put it in the affirmative rather than the interrogative mode:

a) The Qur'an is the Word of God.

b) Jesus Christ is the Word of God.

If both statements are true, then we seem to be landed with the conclusion that the Qur'an (Koran) *is* Jesus Christ. This may seem strange since there seems to be no obvious relationship between the two. Yet both are asserted by divine revelation, and both have been believed in with passionate conviction as being mutually exclusive interpretations of the Word of God as revealed in scripture. And since we have mentioned scripture we may immediately add that the Koran (also called the 'Book' *par excellence*) has a far greater claim to be regarded as scripture than has that heterogeneous collection of writings known as the Bible. Hence, to the unbiased mind, to speak of 'Biblical' religion would logically mean Koranic religion since, as Wilfrid Cantwell Smith rightly points out, the Bible is not the Word of God (in Christianity only Christ is that), but the Koran is. To this elementary point we will return later.

Before discussing the claims of the Koran to be the final revelation which both fulfils and corrects the earlier dispensations of Moses and Jesus, I should like to consider some of the difficulties with which Islam, the religion of the Word made Book, was to confront a later generation of theologians and to compare this with the similar difficulties concerning the Person and nature of the Word made flesh which faced Christian theology from the very beginning. For the purposes of this chapter I will confine myself to Abū Bakr al Kalābādhi, who flourished in the ninth century AD, for three reasons: a) although a Sūfī, he followed the orthodox theory concerning the status and nature of the Koran, b) his summary of the theological issues at stake is refreshingly brief; and c) because an English translation of his principal work is available.[5]

Theology has never plagued Islam to the extent it has Christianity, first because the original impetus of the new religion which was trimphahist from the very beginning was channelled into the conquest of the already decaying Persian Empire and the overrunning of the African and Syriac-speaking provinces of the Roman-Byzantine Empire, and secondly because in the nature of the case no theologian had any part in the transmission of the Word made Book which was directly revealed to Muhammad, God's chosen Prophet, and to him alone. However, once men began to reflect on the new revelation they were bound to ask themselves the question: if the Koran was, as they all believed, God's Word made Book, what was the relationship of God's word or rather his 'speech' (*kalām*) to God? Above all, was it created or uncreated? This might be described as the Muslims' Arian controversy. On the one side you find Christians asking whether Jesus Christ was co-eternal and consubstantial with God; on the other you have the Muslims asking much the same question about the Koran. In fact in the ninth century AD orthodoxy finally swung round to the view that the Koran was uncreated and co-eternal with God, and this has remained the orthodox position ever since.

Given the fact that Muslim theology was from the earliest times in contact with Greek philosophy, one might have supposed that once orthodoxy had declared itself unequivocally in favour of an uncreated Koran the theologians would have felt themselves impelled to clarify this apparent duality in the Godhead as the

Christians had so remorselessly done before them. But they refrained from doing so for two reasons: first, since the Koran is the Word of God made manifest as a Book, your instinct is not to try to explain it (and, as some thought, explain it away) in terms of an alien philosophy. In this the Muslims resembled the Jews, for whom the Torah was the Word of God: the Word of God, if it is to be explained at all, must be explained *by* the Word of God itself and not in terms of an alien philosophy. Hence Al-A'sharī finally won the day with his famous dictum that the Koran was to be accepted *bi-lā kayf* 'without asking how'. This put a stop to further creative theologising (except among the Sūfīs who were a law unto themselves), but it did not abrogate the early theology which orthodoxy had accepted and which had now become official dogma. And among these dogmas was, of course, the uncreated Koran (which is nowhere asserted in the Koran itself) as well as the endlessly repeated Koranic affirmation of the absolute unity of God and the unforgivable impiety of associating anyone or anything with him or even of likening him to anything else at all. You must, then, say that the Koran is the 'speech' of God, and 'speech' is one of the eternal attributes of God, like 'seeing' or 'hearing', but you may not say how this can possibly be so.

Secondly, the Koran itself emphatically discourages interpretation. It repeatedly speaks of the 'Book' (one of the stock names for the Koran itself) as being *mubīn*, 'clear, making clear', almost 'self-explanatory'[6] because it was manifested in plain Arabic speech,[7] in the local vernacular, and not in a sacred language that could not be understood. But, though the language might be clear, what is signified might be anything but clear. In such cases the faithful would do well not to indulge in presumptious interpretation. The warning is clear:

> He (God) it is who sent the Book down to you (Muhammad). In it some verses are clearly formulated: these are the essential part [*umm*] of the Book, but others are ambiguous. As to those whose hearts incline towards deviation, they follow what is ambiguous in it, desiring to stir up trouble, desiring to interpret it. But no one knows its interpretation except God. And those who are firmly rooted in knowledge say: 'We believe in it; all is from our Lord.'[8]

You could scarcely ask for a more emphatic discouragement of theological speculation. Yet theological speculation there had to be, and not least about the Koran itself. The orthodox position is summed up by Al-Kalābādhī in these words:

> They are agreed that the Koran is the Word [*kalām*, 'speech'] of God in very truth and that it is neither created not originated nor a novelty [*hadath*]; yet it is recited on our tongues, written in our copies of it, memorised in our breasts without being localised in any of these. Rather God is known in our hearts, recited on our tongues, worshipped in our mosques without being localised in any of them. They are further agreed that the Koran is neither a body nor a substance nor an accident.[9]

Al-Kalābādhī goes on to argue that the uncreated Koran cannot consist of letters and sounds since it is an eternal attribute of God and as such exempt from all multiplicity and change. The revealed Koran, 'brought down' by the Angel Gabriel who, in the Koran, is identical with the Holy Spirit, *is* composed of letters and sounds, yet even so it remains the eternal Word of God, though how this can be so Al-Kalābādhī totally fails to make clear. All he can say is that 'every Koran except the Word [*kalām*] of God, is originated and created whereas *the* Koran which *is* the Word of God, is neither originated nor created'.[10]

At this point, clearly, we are entering the sphere of mystery. In God the Koran as Word of God is co-eternal with him; but once manifested as speech proceeding from the mouth of Muhammad, it is still eternal as 'speech' but created in so far as this 'speech' or Word is divided into sounds and letters, yet the sum total of these sounds and letters which make up the totality of the Book is still the uncreated Word but now made as intelligible to man as it is possible to make anything eternal comprehensible to a finite mind.

This 'mystery' might usefully be compared to the syllable 'OM' in Hinduism. In eternity it is one single sound, but as manifested among men it appears as the Hindu sacred book, the Veda. In both cases the Sound-Speech-Word is made first Koran (*Qur'an*, meaning 'verbal recitation') and then Book (*kitāb*). This seems natural enough since human beings learn to express themselves first by generalised sounds, secondly by speech proper, and last of all in writing. The Koran then, once it becomes the Book, is the eternal Word of God made as intelligible as possible to literate man.

Again the relationship of the eternal Word of God to the individual copies of the written Koran might be compared with the relationship of the Word made flesh in Christianity to the sacred elements in Holy Communion. Just as Jesus Christ is the Word of God made man according to Christians, so is the Koran the Word of God made Book. On this analogy you might say that, just as Christ is really present in every piece of bread and every drop of wine used in the sacrament of Holy Communion, so is the Eternal Word of God present in every copy of the Koran. The recitation of the Koran is therefore the Muslim sacrament; the man who recites it hears the Word, absorbs it and 'inwardly digests' it and then returns it in thanksgiving to God from whom it eternally proceeds. The *hāfiz*, 'the man who knows the whole Koran by heart', then, almost attains to the dignity of Muhammad, the human vehicle through whom the Word became manifest to man.

But to return to the apparent contradiction between the Word of God made man and the Word of God make Book. Is this contradiction a real one, or is it simply a philological misunderstanding? The Arabic word used for the Word of God (which is the Koran) is *kalām*; the Greek word as applied to Jesus Christ is, as we all know, *logos*. But do they mean the same thing?

In the Koran the word *kalām* means literally the 'word' of God,[11] that is what God says to man. That this 'word' is temporal and not eternal seems undeniable to the rational mind as the passages specifically quoted by Al-Kalābādhī to 'prove' that the Koran is *un*created all too clearly show; for religion, it should be remembered, has nothing whatever to do with reason. What Al-Kalābādhī actually says is this:

Since God has affirmed that speech [*kalām*] belongs to himself in the words 'And God spoke to Moses directly' (*kallama . . . taklīman*) . . . it necessarily follows that this attribute [speech] belongs to him for ever. Were this not so, his speech would be [the same as] that of originated creatures, and in pre-eternity he would have possessed attributes which are the opposite of speech, that is, silence or an impediment [of speech].[12]

As an argument for the uncreated nature of the Koran this is, of course, worse than worthless since the mere fact that God spoke to Moses directly proves that he spoke to him in time and not in some Neo-Platonic 'now'. However, though the arguments used in support of the 'mystery' of the uncreated Koran may be feeble, this mystery still remains central in Islam: the Koran *is* the Word of God, and by 'Word' the Muslims mean what they say, that is the speech that God addresses to man in his sacred books, all of which are summed up in and corrected by his final revelation which is the Koran. The Koran, then, *is* eternal truth, *bi-lā kayf*, meaning that you are to accept this as God-given: it is not yours to ask the reason why.

Islam, then, roundly affirms that the Koran is the eternal Word of God revealed to man in time through the Prophet Muhammad. How, then, can this 'Word' also 'become flesh' in the man Jesus Christ as the Christians maintain?

The translation of the Greek word *logos* as 'Word' which persists even in the New English Bible could scarcely be more inept. Oddly enough, this literalist translation is supported by the Koran itself. Like Adam, Jesus is a special creation brought into existence by God's creative Word *kun*, 'be!' 'In God's sight Jesus is like Adam: he created him from dust, then he said to him "Be!" and he is.'[13] This probably means no more than that Jesus, like Adam, had no earthly father, and the emphasis is on the miraculous nature of his birth: it is as miraculous as the creation of Adam from the dust of the earth. In Jesus's case the word 'dust' is obviously used in a figurative sense since this verse concludes one of the many passages recounting Christ's nativity in the Koran, in which, as in the Gospels, Mary is visited by an angel who brings the glad tidings that she will give birth to a son 'whose name is the Messiah, Jesus, son of Mary, pre-eminent in this world and the next'. As in the Gospels, too, Mary asks how this can come about seeing that no man has touched her, to which the angel replies: 'God creates what he wills. When he decrees a thing, he simply says to it "Be!" and it is.'[14] Jesus, then, is the created incarnation of the divine word 'Be': he is quite literally the Word made flesh.

From the Christian point of view the comparison of Jesus to Adam is interesting, and is probably to be interpreted as a reference to Jesus as the second Adam. Muslims, of course, accuse Christians of idolatry in worshipping Jesus, incarnation of the Word though he is, but, if they are to accept the plain meaning of the Koran, they must concede that the first Adam, before he fell, was a divine being whom God bade the angels worship: 'And they prostrated themselves except only Iblis [the Devil] who refused in his pride and so became an unbeliever.'[15] If it is lawful to worship the first Adam, Christians might well ask, is it not even more appropriate to worship the second, who is 'a word from God'[16] and a 'spirit' from him.[17] However, we are not discussing the Christology of the Koran now, the point at issue being that according to the Koran itself Jesus is literally the Word of God, albeit created; in other words, from the Muslim point of view the uncreated Word of God attests that the created Word of God 'cast upon Mary'[18] is Jesus the Messiah. This might well satisfy any Arians still left among us, but it cannot satisfy orthodox Christians since for them Christ is the one and only Word of God.

The phrase, as applied to Jesus, is, of course, nonsense; and one of the reasons that it is nonsense is that *logos* does not mean 'word'. In the prologue of the Gospel according to St John, as every well educated Christian should know, the Logos is not the 'Word' but the rational principle of the universe, the 'image of the unseen God' of Colossians 1. 15, and the 'radiant light of God's glory and the impress of his very being, sustaining the universe by the word (*rhēma*) of his command', of Hebrews 1. 3. It is the Logos of Philo and the Stoics which ultimately goes back to Heraclitus; and Mr Edward Hussey's translation of it as 'the true account of the law of the universe'[19] would correspond almost exactly to what John means by the Logos. If this is so, and if it were explained to the average Muslim that this is what it meant, it is unlikely that he would be any the wiser. Basing himself on the Koran, he would and often does understand how it is legitimate to say that Jesus is *a* word or *a* spirit from God or even that he is *the* Word of God[20] *par excellence*, just as he is traditionally surnamed *the* Spirit of God by common consent even as Muhammad is surnamed *the* Beloved of God; but were he to be told that the word 'Word' really meant 'the true account of the law of the universe' he would probably think that, in applying this to 'the Messiah, Jesus, son of Mary, pre-eminent in this world and the next', of whom the Koran speaks, the Christians were even more wrong-headed and crazy than he had supposed.

Thus it would appear that without recourse to extreme casuistry it is impossible to reconcile the Christian contention that the Word of God was made man in Jesus Christ with the Muslim (though not Koranic) assertion that the Word of God was made Book in the shape of the Koran. If this is to be done at all, then Christians will have to revert to an Arian position and say that Jesus is the *created* word of God, and the Muslims will have to do likewise: they will have to revive the Mu'tazilite position according to which the Koran is also the *created* word of God. In doing so and thereby rejecting an age-old dogma not authorised in the Koran itself, they would rid themselves of the last trace of an insidious polytheism which they have allowed to creep into their religion; for the Koran, as the Speech of God, is obviously not on the same level as his other attributes – seeing, hearing, power, life, etc., since it is not generalised divine Speech but a book – *the* Book, to be precise, which, as Wilfrid Cantwell Smith has said[21] 'is the eternal life-giving source of the religious life of the continuing community'. As such it has become hypostasised as co-God with God, separate from him in the sense that it is composed of sounds and letters, but identical with him in that it is also – pre-eminently – his eternal Word in Eternity, the creative Word which contains all truth. From the strictly monotheistic point of view, it would seem, the divinisation of the Koran is as objectionable as the divinisation of Jesus.

However this may be (and the case can be argued endlessly on either side), the question still remains that even if both sides were to admit that both 'the Messiah, Jesus of Mary' and the Koran were either separate 'words' of God or the same identical Word variously manifested, it still remains to be decided which 'Word' is to take precedence over the other.

Now, since Christians assert on very slender evidence indeed that Jesus, the incarnate 'true account of the law of the universe', fulfils the Old Covenant entrusted to the Jews in the Torah and developed in the prophets, thereby abrogating the older dispensation, they should be prepared to admit that, owing to their backsliding, quarrelsomeness, and inveterate sinfulness in which they at least equal and possibly excel the Jews, God, in his inscrutable providence, might see fit to send down a final revelation which should reconcile the ferociously differing attitudes of the two parties which centre around the person of Jesus. This is indeed precisely what the Koran does. It vehemently rejects Jewish slanders against Mary and her son, both of whom it treats with a reverence far exceeding that accorded to Moses and the other prophets, and at the same time rebukes the Christians in the strongest possible terms for asserting that God has a son, or (more curiously) that Jesus and Mary are two gods apart from God.[22] As against the Jews, the Koran raises Jesus to a semi-divine status it does not accord to Muhammad himself; it seeks to establish a mean between Jewish calumny and Christian exaggeration. And it is precisely because the 'People of the Book', that is the Jews and Christians, are at loggerheads that a new and final revelation was *necessary*.

This final revelation has come to be known as Islam, a very general term meaning 'submission' (to God). Technically it has come to be applied exclusively to the followers of Muhammad, the 'Seal of the prophets'; but in the Koran it is applied to any true monotheist who preceded the Muhammadan revelation. The true religion was indeed never absent from mankind, but it was truly and authentically present in Abraham who preceded both the Jewish and the Christian dispensations, themselves authentic and true but corrupted by the perversity of their followers. Islam, then, is the *first* religion in that it was the religion of Abraham, as well as the *last* – the definitive revelation granted to Muhammad, which was to fulfil and abrogate all the others and arbitrate between them. The key passage in the Koran in this connexion is perhaps 3. 57–61:

Say: 'People of the Book! Agree upon a formula which we and you have in common, namely, that we serve no one but God, that we do not associate anything with him, and that some of us do not accept others as lords to the exclusion of God.' If they still turn aside, say: 'Bear witness that we submit [to God] [i.e. are Muslims].'

People of the Book! Why do you dispute about Abraham,

seeing that neither the Torah nor the Gospel were sent down until after his time? Have you no sense at all?

It is you who dispute [even] about things of which you have [revealed] knowledge. So why do you dispute about things about which you have no [such] knowledge? Only God knows: you do not.

Abraham was no Jew, nor was he a Christian: he was a simple monotheist [*hanīf*], a Muslim, (one who has submitted to God): he was not one to associate others with God [*mushrik*].

Surely the people who were closest to Abraham are those who followed him, and *this* Prophet [Muhammad] and those who have believed [in him]: for God is the patron of the believers.

There follow three verses which attack the 'People of the Book' for wilfully leading others astray, for refusing to believe in the evident truth of the 'signs' of the new dispensation, and for mixing up truth with falsehood.

The argument here is that Abraham possessed the true monotheism pre-eminently and that this was distorted later by both the Jews and the Christians. Abraham was a true Muslim both in the general sense of one who whole-heartedly submitted to God and in the technical sense of being a Muslim in contra-distinction to the Jews and Christians. There is truth in the beginning, with Abraham; and there is truth at the end, with Muhammad. In the middle, despite the fact that both Moses and Jesus were true prophets, there was error, confusion, and endless wrangling about revelation and even about matters to which human intelligence has no access. One of the functions of the mission of Muhammad, then, was to reintroduce the pure monotheism of Abraham which he hoped would be acceptable to both the Jews and the Christians. It was not: and just as the early Christians attributed the refusal of the bulk of Jewry to accept the new dispensation to sheer obstinacy and ill will, so did Muhammad see the same unamiable qualities in both Jews and Christians. And with far more reason: for, whereas the Koranic revelation can quite reasonably be seen as a divine corrective to the excesses of the Jews and Christians in the matter of Jesus, no wholly rational or wholly unbiased being can honestly see how Christianity, with its obnoxious doctrines of the Incarnation and the Holy Trinity, can possibly be represented as fulfilling anything in traditional Judaism. This has recently been brought out by Dr Geza Vermes in his excellent book *Jesus the Jew*, which, reasonable and closely argued as it is, Christian critics have on the whole been unable to swallow. This is not surprising, since Christian theologians, however 'radical' they may advertise themselves as being, are as indoctrinated in their belief that Jesus Christ is the Son of God and God incarnate (two mutually exclusive ideas, one would have thought) that they cannot see how natural and inevitable the reaction of Jewry was to what it considered to be the monstrous and blasphemous claims made by the new sect; nor can they see how generous and reverent was the treatment accorded to the created Word of God (who is Jesus) by the uncreated Word of God (which is the Koran) according to the Muslim dispensation which was to have set the record straight. Yet none of this seems at all unreasonable.

Again, the Muslims can and do claim that *their* revelation, the true Word made Book, was revealed to the Prophet Muhammad over a period of some twenty years, whereas the definitive text of the divine Book was finally settled by the intervention of the third Caliph 'Uthmān' some thirty years after the Prophet's death. No such claim or anything remotely like it could be made on behalf of either the Old or the New Testament; and the heterogeneous nature of these documents and the spuriousness of some of them have become all the more apparent as a result of the intensive and often captious criticism to which they have been subjected in recent times. The Koran is exempt from this type of criticism at least, since there is no question of multiple authorship, nor has there ever been any dispute as to what is Koran – what is the Word of God – and what were the words of the Prophet, later to be collected separately as the 'traditions of the Prophet'. For once, then, God had spoken plainly in the full light of history; it did not take some four hundred years for the faithful to decide what was Holy Writ and what was not, as in the case of the Christians, whose task was made the more difficult by the fact that their founder left nothing at all in writing. If God, besides being beyond reason, is not also devoid of it, his revelation in the Koran makes some sense. And, free from theology as the Koran is, it even makes simple sense to simple men.

When Christians argue that the Koran's account of Jesus makes no room for their own basic doctrine of the Atonement, they are of course perfectly right; but they fail to see that it is this doctrine above all others that modern man finds both unacceptable and repulsive. According to Islam the sin of Adam did not constitute an absolute break between God and man because Adam was forgiven;[23] hence there was no need for reconciliation, let alone for the bloody sacrifice of a God-Man, the purpose of which was to appease an outraged God. The Islamic God may be capricious, but he is not so apparently outrageous as the Biblical God whose extreme displeasure with the human race can only be mollified by the sacrifice of his own Son.

As to the other Christian criticisms of Islam, two are still very much in the air. First, the Prophet himself permitted polygamy (four wives being allowed to each man), though he himself received a special dispensation from God to exceed this number in any way that pleased him;[24] and secondly he spread the new religion by force of arms. These particular accusations are, of course, perfectly true, and they have in fact influenced educated Muslims to the extent that they have tried to palliate and explain away these two aspects of their faith. They need hardly have done so since, in our modern age of easy divorce, Islam would seem to be very much more at home than is Christianity; for easy divorce (for the husband at least) is part and parcel of the Muslim code. As to polygamy, it is true that the modern world has not got round to this yet, but there would seem to be no good reason why it should not do so. It is only one step from having different wives in rapid succession to having several of them at the same time. In any case, in both respects Islam was merely following ancient Jewish practice; and in the matter of chastity (that one-time virtue which the modern world contemptuously rejects) Muhammad compares very favourably with Solomon and even with David, whose acquisition of Bathsheba by arranging for her husband's death is rarely reckoned to his credit. Indeed, it was strongly condemned by the Lord God himself, but this did not prevent him from receiving David back into his favour. If, as seems certain, the same God is speaking in the Old Testament and in the Koran, then we can be very sure that he would not have withdrawn his favour from Muhammad for his far more trivial offences (if such they were), even if we did not have the evidence of the Word made Book itself that he did so. The God of the Koran is, after all, primarily defined as 'the Merciful, the Compassionate'; he no longer advertises himself as the 'Lord God of Armies', though, of course, he is that too.

And this brings us to our last point, the reproach levelled against Islam, that it, alone among the world religions, took up the sword in order to subdue rather than to convert the infidel by peaceful means as the Buddha had done in India. The accusation is in any case untrue, since the Old Testament Jews were from the beginning commanded by their God to conquer a land which had never been theirs but which he had promised them, and to grant no quarter to the native inhabitants. Jesus, it is true, had rejected the traditional view of the Messiah as the victorious liberator of Israel from gentile domination, but this did not stop his followers from spreading the faith by force once they were strong enough to do so. Muhammad, after suffering persecution in Mecca, was offered supreme power by the citizens of Medina, and he did resort to arms against his old pagan enemies; but it could be argued and indeed is argued by Muslims that this was what we would now call a legitimate 'defensive' war, since the Meccans who had so decisively rejected him in his native town could scarcely have been expected to remain passive spectators while he was busy consolidating his power in Medina.

In the initial struggle the driving-force behind the Muslim armies (and, it must be remembered, these were diminutive) was an absolute faith in the Prophet and the Message he brought from God. The Muslim expansion after the Prophet's death, which can be justly described as the greatest 'miracle' in history, was in fact carried out by fair-weather converts, many of whom had bitterly opposed the Prophet before his final triumph. That the Christians of the Roman Empire and the Zoroastrians of the Persian one embraced Islam *en masse* in a relatively short space of time was no doubt due to a large extent to expediency, since religion has never been the 'ultimate concern' of the majority of mankind, as Paul Tillich would have us believe. Probably rather more than ninety per cent of the human race are always prepared to conform to the current ideology, whether that is Christian, Muslim, Buddhist, Marxist, or Fascist. That the vast majority of Christians overrun by the Muslim armies happily adopted the new faith was due probably much less to coercion than to the fact that they had no difficulty in accepting the new monotheism which was not bedevilled by those intractable mysteries concerning the Person and nature of Christ and the unintelligible doctrine of the Holy Trinity that seemed to bring back polytheism by the back door, but which offered them a God, wholly simple and wholly One, whom they were required to serve reverently and who would infallibly reward their faith on the Day of Judgement. This they could do with the better grace since the new religion did not bid them renounce Jesus, the Messiah, and his mother, Mary, but rather commanded them to hold them in high esteem.

In their assessment of Islam Christians would do well to ponder the wise words of Gamaliel: 'If this idea of theirs or its execution is of human origin, it will collapse; but if it is from God, you will never be able to put them down, and you risk finding yourselves at war with God.'[25]

No one has so far succeeded in putting the Muslims down: *ergo*, according to this Christian text, they are 'from God'.

I am not particularly interested in beguiling bewildered Trinitarians into a purer monotheism since the Muslims themselves might be expected to do this. What I am trying to say, however, is that the Muslim affirmation that the Koran is the Word of God finally and definitively revealed in the Book (where you would expect to find it rather than in human flesh), is eminently reasonable, once you accept a transcendent God who operates in time, is inscrutable and capricious, and quite prepared to change his mind when he thinks fit (for such is the God of prophecy before he fell into the hands of the philosophising theologians). If you are not, then you will have to turn to the God of the philosophers, to the God of Zoroaster, or to no God at all.

Unlike Christianity Islam is a pure monotheism since it rejects all worship of anyone or anything that is not the One God absolutely as being idolatrous. Whether you believe in the real Presence of Christ in the Eucharist or not makes no difference; for to be a Christian at all has, until quite recently, meant to confess Jesus Christ, who is also Jesus of Nazareth, the son of Mary, as Lord and God. For those puritans who see idolatry everywhere, this is surely the ultimate idolatry; and for such as these Islam would seem to be a satisfying answer.

Chapter 7

The God of the Philosopher

'God of Abraham, God of Isaac, God of Jacob, not the God of the philosophers and scientists,' Pascal wrote in ecstasy when for two brief hours he attained what was plainly for him a beatific vision which (as is usual in all the higher mystical states) brought him certainty, joy, and peace. The God he experienced, as he makes abundantly clear, was the God of the prophets, not the God of the philosophers. Though he did not know it, Abraham, Isaac, and Jacob between them may be said to represent the 'types' of the three great monotheistic religions: for did not the followers of Muhammad claim that Abraham was himself a 'Muslim' and the prototype of the historical Muslims who called themselves by this name and attributed it exclusively to themselves as the true heirs of Abraham whose message was now retransmitted in its pristine purity to their own Prophet Muhammad, the 'Seal' of the prophets?

The word 'Muslim', as we have seen, means 'one who submits [to the will of God]'. In this sense Abraham was the first true Muslim – the first uncompromising monotheist – though he founded no religious community. This was left to the later prophets, Moses and Jesus, both of whom founded religious communities of their own, which, in the more general application of the word, could also claim to be 'muslim', but which had, in the course of time, perverted the original pure monotheism of Abraham. With the advent of Muhammad, however, the pure 'Islam' of Abraham had been restored. The first of the ancient patriarchs, then, prefigured the last of the prophetic revelations which had been vouchsafed to Muhammad.

Isaac in his turn might be said to have prefigured the religion of Jesus; for Isaac was Abraham's only son whom God had bidden Abraham sacrifice. Both had 'submitted' to God's terrible command – they had become 'muslims' – but at the last moment Isaac was reprieved and a ram was substituted in his place. Just such a sacrifice was demanded of Jesus, but in his case the father was no human agent but God himself, who, by sacrificing his only Son in human form, sought (for so the incredible story runs) to reconcile an estranged humanity to himself. If, then, Abraham can be seen as representing Islam, Isaac appropriately represents Christianity, while Jacob of course *is* Israel, for so was he renamed by Almighty God. Between them, then, they represent the religion of prophecy in all its fullness. This is the God whom Pascal claimed to have experienced, though the triple association of the three patriarchs with the three religions with which they were loosely connected would have been little to his taste. Be that as it may, he was quite certain that the God who had transported him outside himself was the God of the prophets, *not* of the philosophers. And by the 'philosophers' he must surely have principally understood that philosopher whom St Thomas Aquinas had elevated to the rank of *the* Philosopher, Aristotle, the intellectual father of the West.

It is India's boast that in her tradition philosophy has never been divorced from theology nor theology from religion, for all three are seen to be aspects of man's relationship to the Ultimate, whereas in the West before the rise of Christianity the reverse might be said to have been true. The reason would seem to be that the ancient Greeks never had a sacred book comparable to the Indian *Veda*, which starts with theological mythology and passes on through a magical phase into philosophical theology; nowhere is there any clean break. In Greece, on the other hand, philosophy starts by making a clean break with the mythological view of the word which attributed all that it could not explain to supernatural agencies which seemed to act in a purely arbitrary way: the search for causes had begun.

The difference between the two traditions can, perhaps, be best put in this way. In India the sacred canon of the *Veda* can be clearly divided into three strata – the *Samhitās*, the *Brāhmanas*, and the *Upanishads*. Of the first the earliest as well as the best known is the *Rig-Veda*, which is composed of more than a thousand hymns dedicated to various gods: it is polytheistic through and through as was all early Indo-European religion. No god is as yet supreme, though gradually this supremacy came to be assumed by the god of storm and war and invincible might, Indra; but even he has to fight for his supremacy, which was never undisputed.

The situation corresponds fairly closely to what we find in the *Iliad*, the *Odyssey*, the Homeric Hymns, and Hesiod in Greece; but it never seems to have occurred to the Greeks to make a sacred canon of these highly venerated works. And the reason would appear to be that (apart from the more than questionable morals of the gods they portrayed) they formed no part of a sacred liturgy whereas the *Rig-Veda* did. It was in its own right profoundly sacred, the very voice of the Divine speaking through the mouths of earthly men engaged in the sacred ritual which was itself regarded as the re-enactment of the creative process.

The *Brāhmanas*, that is the strictly sacrificial and magical portions of the sacred canon, need not detain us here since there is nothing at all in ancient Greece which even remotely corresponds to these chaotic and rebarbative texts. All that need be said is that at the very end of them we seem to be struggling out of an atmosphere of sympathetic magic into one of pantheistic mysticism, a kind of mysticism that seems to be based not only on magical identifications of different aspects of the cosmos with different aspects of man but also with a genuine experience of what Romain Rolland[1] called the 'oceanic feeling'. This is the theme (or rather one of the themes) of the most recent stratum of the *Veda* – the Upanishads – in one of the earliest of which we read: 'An ocean, One, the seer becomes, without duality.'[2] Here we already have that mystical apperception of the oneness of all things which has been characteristic of Hinduism ever since. It superseded once and for all the mythological and magical outlook of the earlier works, which from now on were to have little more than an antiquarian interest. Yet along with the Upanishads they still remained sacred; and philosophy in Hinduism at least never succeeded or indeed wanted to succeed in breaking loose from theology. Indeed it was the handmaid of theology in that Scripture (as interpreted by the individual philosopher) remained authoritative, since, to prove his arguments, the philosopher would always appeal to Scripture in his own support. The same, of course, was true of Christian philosophy from the beginning – but with this difference: in Christianity philosophy had to fight against strong 'fundamentalist' opposition in order to be admitted into the new religion at all; for the Bible may be all kinds of things, but it is certainly not philosophy, as Luther discovered to his unspeakable relief. In Hinduism this was not so since philosophy – the inquiry into the nature of things – grew out of the older mythology by questioning it in much the same way as the religion of the prophets of Israel grew out of the Torah by questioning the whole sacrificial cult minutely described therein and demanding a more ethical interpretation thereof more in keeping with the new conception of God as revealed to the prophets themselves, the God who no longer demanded sacrifice but mercy.

In Greece none of this happened. The traditional literature was never transformed into a sacred canon; and, when the questioning came, it came not to complement and 'fulfil' the older ideas but to attack and destroy them. God, these early thinkers considered, if he is to be God at all, must be acceptable to reason, and this was certainly not the case with the gods of Homer and Hesiod, who, as Xenophanes of Colophon, writing in the sixth century BC, rightly pointed out, had 'attributed to the gods everything which brings shame and reproach among men: theft, adultery, and fraud'.[3] Certainly you find frontal attacks on the traditional religion as traditionally interpreted both in the Old Testament and the Upanishads, but in both cases the religious structure was strong enough to incorporate and absorb these new insights and interpret them as an interiorisation of the old. So too Christianity had no difficulty in accepting the Old Testament (which was originally the only 'Scripture' it possessed anyhow) while abrogating the Jewish Law and interpreting the whole document in a way that was both incomprehensible and utterly repugnant to the Jews. In both cases the newer and more ethical forms of religion both complemented and superseded the older, but the older retained its status as the foundation on which the new was to be built.

In Greece, however, there was nothing that corresponded either to the Torah, the 'Law' allegedly dictated by God to Moses on Sinai and therefore sacrosanct, or to the *Rig-Veda*, the 'speech' of God which inspired sages of immemorial antiquity had 'heard' in a form made intelligible to man (for the Sanskrit word *shruti* which is usually translated, as 'revelation' originally meant 'hearing') and therefore equally sacrosanct. Neither the *Iliad* nor the *Odyssey* ascribed to Homer can be described as 'sacred' literature, although they are indispensable source-books for the student of early Greek religion. But there is all the difference in the world between a source-book used by modern scholars to throw light *on* religion and a document which is 'religious' in its own right. Hesiod's *Theogony*, however, describing as it does the genesis of the gods, might be thought to have religious authority in its own right too; but this was not to be, because 'between Hesiod and even the earliest Presocratics there is a great gulf, created by a revolution in thought'.[4] For once the word 'revolution' is correctly used here; for if 'revolution' means anything it means a complete break with the past: things can never be the same again. Just as after the French Revolution there could be no return to the *ancien régime*, although Napoleon and his successors were quite happy to restore the traditional religion (in this case Catholicism) with all its ancient trappings; but they did this because any tradition acts as a conservative force which binds together the existing social structure. In the end he failed because the Catholic Church in France had become so closely identified with the pre-revolutionary monarchy that until quite recent times it had the greatest difficulty in shaking itself free from its strictly feudal past.

Similarly in ancient Greece it might and did seem convenient to keep the local cults devoted to the national deities going, but this was a matter of politics, not of personal religious conviction. True, the Hindus, with their genius for adaptation, to this day see no incongruity between the monistic idealism expressed in its most uncompromising form by the ninth-century philosopher Shankara and what appears to the outsider to be the most childish image worship. The Greeks, however, had no talent for blurring the contours, and could not therefore see the mythological fantasies of Homer and Hesiod as being in some way identical with their new philosophical insights. They could not, as the incarnate god, Krishna, does in the *Bhagavad-Gītā*, roundly condemn the ancient sacrificial religion in one breath only to commend it in the next. The 'God of the philosophers' would have no part in the God of mythology, the Greek equivalent of Pascal's 'God of Abraham, God of Isaac, God of Jacob'. The sharp distinction that Xenophanes makes between the two can best be understood by turning to page 13 of Edward Hussey's excellent little book.[5] There the mythological point of view is pithily expressed in the following aphorisms:

'But mortal men imagine that gods are begotten, and that they have human dress and speech and shape.' They do indeed; and even the unbegotten God of the Old Testament and the Koran is represented as having 'dress and speech and shape', though we are told that these are only to be accepted as figures of speech, or, as the Muslim theologians put it, *bi-lā kayf*, 'without asking how'. Strange too that a begotten God, traces of whom still survive in the Old Testament (those notorious 'sons of God' who married as many of the daughters of men as they thought fit,[6] not to mention Satan who is among their number in the Book of Job (1. 6)), even such a 'begotten' Son of God should appear in the Christian dispensation, thereby, apparently, justifying the pagans to some extent as against the Jewish monotheistic reform.

So far from it being true that man was made 'in the image and likeness of God' as that ancient Jewish story would have us believe, Xenophanes saw clearly, as Feuerbach was to see in modern times (as if he had thought up something new!) that men made their gods in their own image and likeness, so much so that 'the Ethiopians say their gods are snub-nosed and black-skinned, the Thracians that they are blue-eyed and red-headed'. This is, of course, as true of the Christian representations of their own 'begotten' God and his Mother as ever it was of the gods derided by Xenophanes: for this Christian God has taken on 'Thracian', that is European, lineaments; and this has not helped the Christian missionary effort.

To rub home his point Xenophanes adds: 'If oxen and horses had hands to draw with and to make works of art as men do, then horses would draw the forms of gods like horses, oxen like oxen, and they would make these gods' bodies similar to the bodily shape that they themselves each had.' If so, they would show themselves rather more sensible than man, who has not hesitated to conceive of his gods in animal or half-animal forms, as he did in ancient Egypt and still does in modern India. 'So powerful', indeed, 'has religion been to convince men of evil (or should we say just "silly") things,' as Lucretius so aptly put it.[7]

If, then, these are the gods of 'religion', what of the 'God of the philosophers'? Here again Xenophanes obligingly supplies the answer:

One God there is, greatest among gods and men, in no way like mortal creatures either in bodily form or in the thought of his mind.
The whole of him sees, the whole of him thinks, the whole of him hears.
He stays always motionless in the same place; it is not fitting that he should move about now this way now that.
But, effortlessly, he wields all things by the thought of his mind.

Someone, at last, seems to be talking sense. Here, in a nutshell, you have the God of the philosophers and of those theologians who use philosophy to explain away the wild paradoxes of their individual revelations. As in the Koran God is 'totally Other', and anything we may say about him can only be by way of analogy. If he sees and thinks and hears, then this is in a way that far transcends our own seeing and thinking and hearing. Being eternal he must be motionless, that is not susceptible to change in any form; yet though changeless himself 'he wields all things by the thought of his mind', that is to say like Aristotle's Unmoved Mover, while unchanging himself he is the ultimate source of all change, or, in the words of the *Brihadāranyaka* Upanishad (3.7.3–23), he is the 'Inner Controller' who, though distinct from all contingent beings, nevertheless indwells them and controls them: 'He is the Self within you, the Inner Controller, the Immortal.'

Such, then, is the God of the philosophers. He has three aspects: first, he is changeless and therefore immortal, being subject to neither birth nor death, coming-to-be or passing away, increase or diminution; second, he is alive and conscious in his whole being; and third, he is the power that directs and orders the whole universe. Above all he is rational and quite free from any arbitrariness which is so characteristic of the ancient gods of both Greece and India and even more so of the Semitic God of the Bible and the Koran. Being impassible he knows nothing of grace, nothing of wrath: he has no favourites and no enemies. If you like, he is just and righteous; he is 'just right', the 'always so', as the Taoists put it.[8] He is the Brahman of the Upanishads.

In the Upanishads the term 'Brahman', the etymology of which is still much disputed, seems originally to have meant something like 'holy power' with connotations of 'right order' (if we are to take the Iranian evidence into account),[9] but in the Upanishads it had come to be used as the stock word denoting the Absolute – also called the 'Self', the inmost and unchanging essence, that is, both of the universe and of individual men. As such it superseded the more concrete identifications of the ultimate principle with 'food' (meaning perpetually changing matter), breath (the breath of life which, breathed out at death, continues to live in the all-pervading wind,[10] mind, space or whatever. To emphasise its superiority to all these and its unlikeness to them it is finally designated as 'the Real of the real'.[11]

All this is very reminiscent of the Presocratics who tended at first to identify this 'Real of the real' with some physical element, Thales with water, Heraclitus with fire, Anaximander with the 'unbounded' and so on. But each philosopher had his own distinct view, none of them so simplistic as they would seem, as Edward Hussey has so convincingly shown. The reverse is true of the Upanishads; and it might well be said that all (or nearly all) of the views of the Presocratics are to be found mixed up higgledy-piggledy throughout the Upanishads. Moreover, the magical and mythological element is by no means absent and was to return in full force later, when personal deities, often half forgotten, suddenly emerged as personal manifestations of the impersonal and unmanifest Absolute. The break had never been complete.

In Greece the break *was* complete: only Zeus, the One God, who is yet at the same time 'the greatest among the gods and men', was retained, since he came to be regarded as being synonymous with *the* God, 'that which truly *is* (*to ontōs ōn*)' as Plato was to say. Plato, it is true, invented a rich mythology of his own which he develops principally in the *Timaeus* and the tenth book of the *Laws*, but in this respect he was scarcely typical; and the God of the philosophers whom *the* Philosopher, Aristotle, thought he had discovered through the natural sciences, through the human sciences (the modern jargon for what he called 'ethics' and 'politics'), and through metaphysical speculation, which was the crown of the other two, had to wait for the coming of an obscure son of a carpenter in Nazareth before it was once more deluged with a mythology both far more amazing and far more gripping than anything the old mythologies had to offer. In the long run philosophy had to come to terms with it though it met with the fiercest resistance from the purists, who wished to preserve their strangely barbaric myth of a humanly divine and divinely human sacrifice, the foundation of which was in the eyes of the uninitiated the death by crucifixion of this same carpenter's son turned rabbi. But the purists lost out to a man of towering genius who, Jew though he was, was nonetheless Hellenised enough to see in this carpenter's son miraculously raised from the dead (as he and all early Christians unshakeably believed to the point of accepting martyrdom with joy) the 'Son' and 'Word' of God himself, 'the image of the unseen God and the first-born of all creation',[12] that is to all intents and purposes the 'Logos' of Heraclitus and the 'Nous' (intellect, mind, consciousness, awareness) of Anaxagoras, Plato, and Aristotle. The process did not stop here since the carpenter's son, Jesus, was increasingly forgotten in favour of the pre-existent principle of rationality (*logos*) with which he had been identified, so that, with Augustine, Christianity becomes Christian Platonism and, with Aquinas, Christian Aristotelianism rather than Platonic or Aristotelian Christianity; for in Aquinas at least *the* Philosopher – Aristotle – is treated with quite as much respect as *the* Apostle – Paul.

It remained for Luther to denounce Aristotle and demand that his pernicious rationalism be banished from the schools and to revile reason itself as a whore – but all in vain, since Protestant theology, though claiming to be 'biblical', very soon lapsed into liberalism, and its revival under the aegis of the prolix and wearisome Karl Barth now looks like a relic from the past. So successful have our modern theological whizz-kids been in demythologising the Jesus of the Gospels that the carpenter's son has disappeared from view and has been transformed into a curious entity called the 'Christ event', which may possibly mean something but is wonderfully unhelpful. Philosophy has fared no better, and particularly that branch of it which Aristotle called 'first philosophy', that is the search for the 'Real of the real' beyond the relatively real which Aristotle called 'appearances' ('phenomena' = Greek *phainomena*, meaning 'things which appear'). But that is another and more depressing story. So let us retrace our steps and consider in a little more detail the 'middle' period in Greek and Indian philosophy – the 'theological' period, if you like – represented by the Prezocratics on the one hand and the Upanishads on the other.

That the Upanishads represented no conscious break with the past has already been noticed: hence they are collectively referred to as the *Vedānta*, 'the end and consummation of the Veda'. Since they form part of the Veda, then, they are equally inspired and not an independent revelation: they simply make explicit what was all along implicit in the earlier revelation. Or, to put it another way, they bring out the inner meaning of a mythological tradition revealed (in much the same way as Christians would have us believe that the Old Testament was revealed) to men not yet mature enough to grasp the full truth. This method was quite foreign to the new thinking in Greece; these thinkers made no effort to find esoteric truths behind the boisterous and capricious behaviour of Homer's immortals or the homicidal genealogies of Hesiod's *Theogony*; they rejected them out of hand and made a new start. The result was that they not only threw up 'natural philosophers' (primitive 'physicists') but also men of a decidedly prophetic stamp of mind who claimed a divine revelation communicated directly to themselves and quite independent of the fairy-tales of the past. Of such were Heraclitus, Parmenides, and the misty figure of Pythagoras, who alone of the three can be regarded as having founded a religious community which modelled its life on what it conceived his teaching to be. The teachings of all three of them are paralleled in the Upanishads, but their teachings are quite distinct whereas in the Upanishads they are gloriously mixed up together.

As we have seen, in one thing the ancient Greeks and Hebrews agreed, and that was in their despair of an afterlife: at best it did not exist, at worst it was a bleak form of existence, for 'the dead know nothing; no more reward for them, their memory has passed out of mind';[13] or, in the chilling words of Achilles when he comes face to face with the living Odysseus in the underworld: 'it is better to live even as the hireling of a poor farmer than to rule over the kingdom of the dead.'[14] These

depressing views of the afterlife which both the Greeks and the
Hebrews owed to the ancient Mesopotamians were never typical
of India. For the earliest Hindus believed, as their Iranian
cousins did, that human life, though discarnate, continued much
as before after death, except that the virtuous (that is those who
had fulfilled their religious duties) could expect a life of
irresponsible pleasure not unlike that of the Homeric gods or the
sensuous joys the Koran reserves for the true believer in paradise,
while the fate of the wicked is left in doubt by the earliest texts,
though the later ones consign them to blind darkness or some
equally depressing form of existence.[15]

These views which were further elaborated in a moralistic
sense by the Zoroastrians in Iran may be regarded as a common
Aryan inheritance in which both Iranians and Indians shared,
but they were soon to be overshadowed by what must have been
the aboriginal doctrine of the transmigration of souls, which,
though it only makes its appearance in Hinduism in the
Upanishadic period, was already taken for granted by the
'heretical' Buddhists and Jains who must then be regarded as
carrying on an already long-established tradition. The Hindus
too, once they had received this virus into their own system,
never got rid of it, so much so that in later days salvation meant
for them, quite as much as for the Buddhists and Jains, not the
prolongation of earthly life in a blissful and immortal state from
which suffering, disease, and old age had been for ever banished,
but the cessation of mortal life altogether, since there is no
such thing as a happy life, life itself being a perpetual state of
anxiety and unease. It is, then, clear enough where the Indian
branch of the Indo-Iranian family derived these depressingly
inhuman ideas. That the Greeks should have acquired them at
all, however, is much harder to explain.

The earliest Greek philosophers, as we have seen, had turned
their back on religion and had sought to discern a rational
pattern behind the universe: they were 'physicists', not
'spiritualists'. With the advent of Pythagoras and the Pythagoreans
all that was to change. Two doctrines were suddenly to appear
which were totally new: the transmigration of souls and the
kindred idea that the immortal soul is the unwilling prisoner
of a mortal, detestable, and filthy body. Salvation can only
consist in being rid of the body once and for all so that the

soul may return to its true home which is immortal and immaterial spirit. This view of human nature may be regarded as the 'orthodox' Indian view which was accepted by the Buddhists and the Jains from the beginning, and adopted by the Hindus at about the same time that the Buddha lived and never again rejected. In the original Graeco-Hebrew view neither was the misery of repeated living and repeated dying accepted nor was there any expectation of an ecstatic release from the dreary round. Man lived but once, and the only immortality he could expect was a vicarious one, either by continuing his line (a course open to everyone since, it would seem, copulation is natural to man), or by leaving a fair name behind him (the Greek way), or by submitting to the will of God (the Hebrew way), or by making the best of what God has given you by eating and drinking and having a good time[16] while paying lip-service to God's commandments the while[17] (the way of Ecclesiastes and the majority of mankind always and everywhere). This was the Graeco-Hebrew orthodoxy which accepted the human condition as it found it, accepting the good with the bad and the inevitability of death which blots out consciousness in 'eternal rest'. This too, it may be mentioned in passing, was also the Chinese orthodoxy whether Confucian or Taoist. It is the line of least resistance – *islām* in the sense of 'submitting' to things as they are – or at least as they appear to be.

The opposite view which became the Indian 'orthodoxy' did not accept the unity of man as an indissoluble compound of body, life, and consciousness, all of which disintegrated at death, but insisted that consciousness or the 'soul' was a stranger imprisoned in the body and could survive the body's death. In proof of this was adduced the phenomenon of dream and the Shamanistic experience in which the soul seems to leave the body while it is yet alive and soars aloft or dives below into regions not normally accessible to man.

The homelands of Shamanism are usually believed to be central and northern Asia, but signs of Shamanistic soul-flights also appear in the Upanishads where any direct influence from Central Asia seems most improbable. These verses, for instance, from the *Brihadāranyaka* Upanishad (4.3.11–13) surely point to such a Shamanistic experience:

By sleep he mashes down the things of body;
Unsleeping, the sleeping [senses] he surveys:
White light assuming, back to his [former] state
He returns – the Golden Person, lonely swan.

Guarding his lower nest with the breath of life,
Forth from the nest, immortal, on he flies.
Wherever he will, immortal, on he goes –
   The Golden Person, lonely swan!

In the realm of dream, aloft, beneath, he roams,
A god – how manifold the forms he fashions!
With women he takes his pleasure, laughs – or else
Sees dreadful sights: so does it seem to him.

There are some who see his pleasure-grove:
   Him no one sees at all!

According to this view such a man is indeed dead while yet
alive: the soul has left the body (the 'lower nest') and there is
always a danger that it will not return. Hence you should never
awake a sleeper suddenly, for 'hard to cure is the man to whom
this [person] does not return'.[18]

All this is grist to the mill of the Upanishads, nor need we
look for any foreign intrusion; for the Upanishads themselves
had an obsession with sleep and dream as being the harbingers
of dreamless sleep and death of the human shell itself. And this,
so far from being a disaster, was accounted a blessing since
the death of the individual consciousness meant its absorption
into the universal consciousness through which it 'became
Brahman', thereby identifying itself with the All.

In the Greek setting, however, the sudden appearance of such
outlandish ideas cries aloud for an explanation. As we have seen,
the most likely source of these ideas is central Asian Shamanism,
which appears to have made its way into Greece via Scythia and
Thrace, though perhaps Pythagoras himself should be credited
with having arrived at the idea of reincarnation independently.[19]

Meanwhile, alongside the official cults, new religious movements
were streaming into Greece, foremost among which was the cult
of Dionysius with which the Orphic mysteries seem to have been
associated. The Dionysian cult, as any reader of Euripides'
deeply disturbing play, the *Bacchae*, very soon comes to realise,
was one which deliberately aimed at 'self-transcendence': it

deliberately sought ecstasy – it took you out of yourself – but what it took you into might be quite as demonic as it was divine. Not surprisingly so, since Dionysius himself shared the attributes of a god and a devil. So long as the orgy lasted the individual's normal personality was replaced by another collective personality which seemed to animate the whole orgiastic group, itself being identified with the spirit of the god himself. The technical term for this was *enthousiasmos*, Anglicised as 'enthusiasm', but literally meaning 'en-godded-ness' or 'possession by a god'. But if so, by what god? Scarcely Pascal's prophetic God, and certainly not the 'God of the philosophers' who was already taking shape in the finest minds of contemporary Greece. Rather it was the ecstatic god of the 'companies of the prophets' mentioned in the Old Testament, with whom the hapless Saul associated,[20] the god of intoxication and ecstasy who inspired that wing of mysticism conventionally described by the Muslims as 'drunken', whose behaviour was akin to madness. In Islam they were described as '*Uqalā al-majānin*, 'sober-drunks', men so far advanced in mystical ecstasy that it had pleased God to release them from all their formal religious and moral duties.

This can be very dangerous since their God (like the God of the higher prophecy of the Old Testament and the Koran itself) is beyond good and evil, and the 'engodded' man can never be sure which side of this two-faced God will come out on top. The *Bacchae* of Euripides supplies the terrifying and deeply ambiguous answer; for this orgiastic God, no less than the 'jealous' God of Israel, demands due worship, and woe to the man or woman who denies it to him. For if you defy him he will possess you in no spirit of kindness but will drive you out of your mind so that you may well dismember your own son under the illusion that he is a lion and you yourself a god, as Agave did to her unbelieving son Pentheus.

All this may seem irrelevant to the God of the philosophers, let alone the God of *the* Philosopher, Aristotle: but it is not, for there can be no doubt that the towering genius who was his teacher, Plato, was deeply influenced by this divine madness,[21] and Aristotle could no more leave Plato's 'enthusiasm' out of account than he could the theory of ideas which he came so thoroughly to dislike.

The new doctrine did indeed present a totally new problem; for if it was true that the soul could, even when the body was alive, pursue a life of its own outside the body, and if that life is infinitely more free and therefore happy, then disembodied life must be infinitely preferable to embodied life, and life itself must become a burden. What point, then, is there in cultivating virtue? Plato answered the question by combining the doctrine of reincarnation which he certainly got from the Pythagoreans with the doctrine of rewards and punishments in after-death states which he may perhaps have derived from Zoroastrian sources. Final beatitude, however, consisted in returning to the world of pure, changeless 'Ideas' from which the soul was supposed to have fallen into this vile body. How Aristotle tackled this problem we shall soon see.

But Pythagoras, as we have seen, was not the only prophet to have arisen in Greece in the sixth century: there was also the 'darkling'[22] Heraclitus and the far more formidable Parmenides, the prophet of the absolute oneness of Being to the exclusion of all becoming. In my last book, *Our Savage God*, I devoted quite a lot of space to the closeness of the thought of these two apparently wholly original thinkers to the two main philosophical trends in the Upanishads – the monistic and the pantheistic – and I have no wish to repeat myself here. I must content myself with giving a very brief account of their thought insofar as it affected Aristotle.

Heraclitus has been claimed as the father of dialectical thinking as understood by Hegel and Marx.[23] That his name should be coupled with that of Aristotle in this context would hardly have pleased the latter since he accused Heraclitus not only of obscurity but also of being arrogant enough to suppose that his own opinions accurately reflected the truth.[24] Moreover, Heraclitus is the master of unresolved paradox, and there are few things that exasperated Aristotle more than this.

Heraclitus has the distinction not only of being the father of 'dialectical' thinking as understood by Hegel and Marx but also of being the first thinker, so far as we know, to have used the word *logos* to mean 'the true account of the law of the universe' as Edward Hussey admirably renders it. As we all know, this Logos, this 'true account of the law of the universe', became a key concept in Christianity: 'In the beginning was the Logos':

'In the beginning was the true account of the law of the universe.' This makes sense as the traditional rendering, 'In the beginning was the Word', does not. Heraclitus, then, has the double distinction of being not only the father of the Hegelian dialectic but also the stepfather of Johannine Christianity. He saw himself as a prophet; and, like all prophets, he speaks in riddles: 'The prince whose the oracle of Delphi is neither tells nor conceals: he gives a sign.'[25] This is precisely how Heraclitus saw himself: like Muhammad he was the vehicle of the 'Word', he was not the Word itself. Nor did he see himself as the 'Word', the 'true account of the law of the universe', made flesh, but as the 'flesh' through which the oracular 'Word' made itself known. This is a doctrine which seems to be strikingly similar to that of the two natures united in the one Person of Jesus Christ. Hence he can say: 'Having heard not me, but the *logos*, it is wise to concur that all is one.'[26] And this too would seem to be a more generalised version of Christ's prayer for his disciples: 'Father, may they be one in us, as you are in me and I am in you.'[27] But for Heraclitus this is no prayer: it is the truth behind all appearances as it is in the Upanishads; but it is a truth that only the initiate can begin to understand:

'Of this *logos* which is always so men prove to have no understanding both before they have heard it and immediately on hearing it; though everything comes to be according to this *logos*, they are like persons who have no experience of it.'[28]

So too the *Katha* Upanishad (2.8) says:

> How difficult for man, though meditating much,
> To know Him from the lips of vulgar men:
> [Yet] unless another tells of Him, the way to Him is barred,
> For than all subtleties of reason he is more subtle:
>   Logic he defies.

To understand the pantheistic 'truth' that 'all is one' you must either have insight yourself or obtain it through the oracular utterances of a guru, in this case Heraclitus. When once you have realised that *in yourself* 'all is one', you can then say with the Upanishad: ' "I am this [the universe]; I am all". That is the highest state of being. This is that form of his which is beyond desire, free from evil, free from fear.'[29]

But if 'all is one' and can be experienced as being one, in what sense can this be true? To this Heraclitus replies with yet another whopping paradox: in the One which is also the All, all the opposites not only meet and are reconciled but are also seen to be *identical*. 'Conjunctions: wholes and not wholes, the converging and the diverging, the consonant and the dissonant, from all things one, and from one all things.'[30] And even more disturbing: 'But one must know that war is universal, and that justice *is* strife, and that all things happen according to strife and necessity.'[31] God himself is the sum total of all the opposites and at the same time their *logos*, 'the true account of the law of the universe', that reconciles the opposites which, though depressingly real to us, are nevertheless only appearances which conceal the ultimate unity and the *logos* and *Nous* ('Mind') that lie behind them.

None of these obscurities satisfied Aristotle since to say that 'all is one' and that everything is the *same* as its opposite seems to be plain nonsense if, as Heraclitus himself says, there is order and mind behind all the discordant appearances. As the proposition stands, of course, it *is* nonsense or, if you prefer it, paradox (for all mystics glory in paradox), but it is possible to make some sense even of paradox, and this is precisely what Aristotle tries to do. Hence he takes up this particular paradox of Heraclitus and says:

> If all existent things are one by definition . . . we will be brought back to Heraclitus' paradox: being good and being bad will be exactly the same as will being not good and being good; which amounts to saying that a good thing and a thing that is not good are exactly the same, and so are a man and a horse. And so we shall no longer be saying that all existent things are one but that they are nothing, and that to possess a certain quality is the same as being of a certain size.[32]

According to this way of thinking anything can be identified with anything else, and this is precisely what the Upanishads do; and that they should do so is extolled as some kind of higher wisdom by their more loose-minded admirers. Yet despite their recklessness it *is* possible for 'one' at the same time to be 'many' in that one substance can possess many attributes. The ancient philosophers had got into difficulties on this subject because they had not been able to draw the necessary distinctions. Though they did not know how, they 'had to admit that the one is many – as if it were inadmissible for the same thing to be both one and many, provided, of course, that they are not diametrically opposed [as are Heraclitus' oppositea]; for the one is one either potentially or actually.'[33]

The concepts of potentiality and actuality which have become part and parcel of our ordinary speech we owe almost entirely to Aristotle and they are basic to his whole philosophy. They and their twin sisters, matter and form, Aristotle used in his valiant effort to show how Being is not incompatible with becoming any more than the eternal is with the transient. That he should have thought it necessary to elaborate this theory at all was due not so much to the sharp distinction that the Pythagoreans, with Plato in their wake, had drawn between spirit and matter, soul and body, as to the fact that the third of these Presocratic prophets, Parmenides, had, like Heraclitus, struck out an entirely new line of his own: and this too is closely paralleled in early Hindu philosophy and has ever since been regarded by the majority of Hindu philosophers as being the highest wisdom.

This is pure monism (or 'non-dualism' as they prefer to call it), an extreme form of idealism which asserts that Being is One, whole, complete in itself, and indivisible, all multiplicity and all becoming being pure moonshine born of the collective and cosmic ignorance of man. This extreme doctrine which asserts that what *is* cannot change or become other than it is, is not by any means maintained throughout the Upanishads, the more general view being that Brahman or the 'Self', which is the Absolute, while remaining 'One without a second' in itself, nevertheless somehow gives rise to and pervades the phenomenal universe while the 'Real of the real' remains One only.

> Descry This with your mind:
> Herein there is no diversity at all:
> Death beyond death is all the lot
> Of him who sees in This what seems to be diverse.
>
> Descry It in its Oneness,
> Immeasurable, firm,
> Transcending space, immaculate,
> Unborn, abiding, great:
>   [This is] the Self.[34]

The vision of eternal Being which is absolutely One and over against which all else is as nothing is never clearly and precisely stated in the Upanishads. In Parmenides it *is* so stated and with a dogmatism far more assured than that of Heraclitus; but his prophetic message is the exact opposite of that of his rival. For Heraclitus God is identical with the universe, the unifying link between the opposites which make it seem such a restless and clashing flux; of this he may be said to be the 'Inner Controller'. For Parmenides, on the other hand, 'God' is the Absolute existing alone and sublimely aloof from the universe which is simply a delusion of man's finite (and therefore non-existent!) mind. That Parmenides considered he derived his 'true knowledge' from a divine source is made clear enough in the arresting prologue that introduces his astonishing poem. In it the prophet sees himself transported in a chariot, escorted 'into the light [by] the daughters of the sun, leaving the halls of Night, and thrusting aside with their hands the veils from their heads. There is the gate of the paths of Night and Day.'[35]

The allegory seems plain enough. The 'daughters of the sun' represent that element of illumination without which all purely mortal opinions must be false. It is what Aristotle was to call in one context the *poiētikos nous*, the 'creative mind' and in another the 'thinking of thinking', that is the divinely active principle which makes correct thinking possible, 'the unthought thinker, the ununderstood understander'[36] of the Upanishads. Night and Day clearly represent truth and untruth as expounded in the main body of the poem itself, the 'truth' being baldly stated as '[it] is', 'untruth' as '[it] is not', while the gate itself may perhaps represent 'the opinions of mortal men in which there is no truly convincing force' shortly to be mentioned, which stands halfway between the two.

Once through the gate of ambiguity with its 'large *double* doors' the prophet is welcomed by the goddess of Justice in these words:

Young man . . . no bad destiny is it that sent you out to come this way – it is indeed a way remote from the paths of men – but that which is right and just. You are to learn everything: both the immoveable heart of well-rounded truth, and the opinions of mortal men, in which there is no truly convincing force – still, that too you shall learn, how these opinions are to cover everything in acceptable fashion.

In the event Parmenides describes two possible paths to true knowledge, neither of which corresponds to the 'opinions of mortal men', because they are represented as two ontological extremes with no middle ground between them.

'Come then,' the goddess says, 'I will tell . . . the ways of inquiry which alone are to be thought of: the first, that says that [it] is and that it cannot be that [it] is not – this is the path of true persuasion, for it follows the truth; the second, that says that [it] is not and that it must be that [it] is not – *this* track, I tell you, is quite undiscoverable. For you could neither know what is not . . . nor speak of it; for whatever is to be spoken of or thought, must *be*; for "to be" *is;* but "nothing" [*mēden*] simply is *not* [*ouk*]. . . . From *this* path, then, of inquiry first I block you.'[37]

In other words, for Parmenides there are two ontological possibilities: (a) [it] *is*, and (b) [it] *is not*. The second is excluded because absolute non-existence is unthinkable, for once you have thought it, it in some sense *is*. Hence you have to accept the only alternative offered you: '[it] *is*', because to 'be' is the one thing that is thinkable apart from any foolish 'opinions' we may derive from our highly fallible senses. After much fumbling the same conclusion was reached in India and was expressed in almost identical terms:

> He cannot be apprehended
> By voice or mind or eye:
> How then can it be understood
> Unless we say just '*is*'.[38]

However, you can say a little more than that as Parmenides himself does: for 'what *is* is ungenerated and indestructible, whole, unique, unmoved, and perfect; nor was it, nor will it ever [come to] be, since it *is* all together, now, one, and coherent.'[39] In other words, in absolute Being there is neither time nor space, no becoming and no change of any kind. All this emerges from the Upanishads too; for this is in essence the 'God of the philosophers'. What is at issue is what his relationship (if any) to our everyday world of appearance can be. From the point of Parmenides' 'truth', obviously none, since the everyday world *is not* absolutely: therefore it does not exist at all. This bleakest of all truths, however, must remain quite incomprehensible and quite unacceptable to 'ignorant mortals, the two-headed creatures . . . [who] drift along, deaf and blind, in confused throngs, like men amazed.'[40] 'Ignorant mortals', of course, means you and me. In order to sweeten this bitterest of 'ontic' pills – *is* – which leaves no room for 'am' and 'are' ('I' and 'you'), the 'truth' had to be diluted in order to be swallowed at all. The only way that Parmenides, along with the Hindus and Buddhists, could do this was to posit two distinct levels of knowledge, the absolute (true) and the relative (false).

In India the idea was first enunciated in the *Mundaka* Upanishad (1.4–5): 'There are two kinds of knowledge which should be known . . . a higher and a lower. Of these the lower consists of the four Vedas, phonetics, ritual, grammar, etymology, and astronomy. The higher is that by which the Imperishable can be understood.' Transmuted into Buddhist terms we find the same principle enunciated by Nāgārjuna, the Buddhist philosopher who flourished shortly after the beginning of the Christian era. For him 'the teaching of the doctrine laid down by [all] the Buddhas is based on two truths, namely, worldly [empirical] truth and absolute Truth. Those who do not recognise the distinction between these two truths do not understand the quintessence of the Buddha's teaching.'[41] Again no link between the upper level and the lower one; but you can never be sure, for, in the obscurity stakes, Nāgārjuna would seem to have the edge over the 'darkling' Heraclitus himself.

So too Parmenides, with a truly Buddhist compassion for men, those 'two-headed' creatures who after all *are not*, allows them 'two forms, *one* of which they should not name' because they assume it to exist apart from the other,[42] whereas in reality only the 'Other' exists. All the rest, as the *Chāndogya* Upanishad (6.1.4–6) insists, which may appear as 'modifications' of Being, are really only 'verbalisations, mere names': the only reality is Being. This, then, is the 'God of the philosophers' at his 'highest' and most uncompromisingly aloof. The task that Aristotle set himself was to bridge the yawning chasm that seemed to have opened between absolute Being (which is God) and nothingness,

which in practice means the universe in which we appear to
live as well as ourselves who (wrongly) believe ourselves to *be*.
How did he set about this?   archetype

For Aristotle philosophy must start from the concrete individual
thing, not from the intuitively apprehended Idea, whether it be
the One of Parmenides or Plato's Idea of the Good. It is the
common experience of everyone that they do in fact exist, and
that they exist in an objective world the reality of which is
attested by the fact that everyone whose senses are not impaired
experiences it in much the same way. This does not mean that
either the individual self or the phenomenal world exist in an
absolute sense, but it does mean that they exist (they *are*) in
some sense – and no philosopher is more tentative and less
dogmatic than Aristotle, for what he is doing is to follow the
'way of opinion' so cavalierly dismissed by Parmenides in order
to arrive through it and not in spite of it at the 'immovable
heart of well-rounded truth', the sole reality of which Parmenides
had prophetically proclaimed. To this end even 'the opinions of
mortal men', 'deaf and blind' though they well might be, as
Parmenides opined, must be taken into account. Since, then, it
is the common opinion of mankind that something immortal
exists which transcends the passage of time (call it 'God' or
'the gods', it does not matter very much which at this stage), it is
reasonable to suppose that this universally shared belief has some
validity, disbelief in the gods being a rather new-fangled Greek
affair.

'All men', Aristotle says, 'have some idea about gods, and all
of them, whether foreign or Greek (at least as many of them as
admit the existence of gods) assign the highest place to the divine,
supposing, obviously, that what is immortal [here] is interconnected with what is immortal [there].'[43] What he means is
that not only do all men have some conception of gods but they
also assign the highest place at least to the most important of them.
'God' then will *naturally* dwell in heaven, though the divine in
general (the minor gods) may well be located elsewhere. In any
case 'immortal is interconnected with immortal' both in the sense
that there are obvious correspondences between the Greek,
Egyptian, and Near-Eastern gods and in the sense that, as
Parmenides puts it, the Divine, though One, is also 'coherent'
or 'continuous': it is, if you like, an eternal continuum. This

applies as much to popular belief as it does to Aristotle's own view of the divine; for just as Zeus dwells in highest heaven, so is Aristotle's own Unmoved Mover situated (if that is the right word) beyond the physical universe, beyond space and time. But God is also present *in* the universe, and in this respect he can be identified with natural law or with Nature itself; for, as Aristotle says, 'God and Nature make nothing to no purpose.'[44] God, however, is clearly distinct from Nature in that it is elsewhere said that Nature *does* make mistakes. From Aristotle's point of view, however, it would be absurd to attribute error to God. And Nature too only makes mistakes – only 'sins' (for to 'sin' in Greek is to 'be mistaken') – in the sublunary world in which we live: in the outer spheres beyond the moon everything works with clockwork precision, for 'nothing appears to have changed either in the whole of outermost heaven or in any of the parts proper to it'.[45]

Here on earth, however, things are different, since Nature herself, like man who is part of her, is liable to error. Indeed:

> Mistakes *are* made even in the crafts and professions. A grammarian may make a mistake in writing and a doctor may prescribe a wrong medicine. Hence it seems clear enough that mistakes can be made in the order of Nature. If, then, there are occasions when, in the exercise of their speciality, professional men and craftsmen achieve their purpose in the right way, and if, when mistakes occur, whatever was attempted was done for some [purpose] but failed to come off, so too something similar must obtain in the sphere of Nature as a whole. And so monsters will be failures of purpose in Nature itself.[46]

The popular cult of the gods was no doubt crude, but it was not for that reason to be discouraged, because though it may have been degenerate, it did at least point to the truly divine of which all mankind has *some* inkling. Aristotle would have certainly concurred with what Krishna, the incarnate God of the *Bhagavad-Gītā* (9.23–4) says about the worship of 'false' gods:

> Even those who devote themselves lovingly to other gods and sacrifice to them, fulfilled with faith, do really worship me though the rite may differ from the norm. For it is I who of

all sacrifices am the recipient and Lord; but they do not know me as I really am, so they fall [back into the world of men].

So too Aristotle is quite happy to tolerate the national and local cults devoted to gods depicted in human or even animal form since, if gods exist other than the Unmoved Mover and his subordinate 'movers', it is reasonable to suppose that they bestow not only good fortune[47] but also beatitude (*eudaimonia*),[48] since this is their own habitual state. Or perhaps he means more than this; for 'if, as seems likely, the gods *are* interested in human affairs',[49] then this must surely apply too to the one true God, the Unmoved Mover, who is himself supremely lovable. Aristotle never says this in so many words because his God, being totally sufficient unto himself, has no need to love us in return. Hence, though the possibility is not excluded, Aristotle was too modest a man to expect any such thing, for the truly unselfish lover loves without expecting anything in return. Of his own Unmoved Mover and the subordinate movers who animate the heavenly spheres which are *his* 'gods' you can only say this:

A tradition has been handed down from the very earliest times and bequeathed to posterity in the form of a myth, namely, that these [movers of the spheres] are gods and that the divine encompasses all Nature. The rest was added later in the form of myth so as to accord with the beliefs of the common people and as a constitutional and utilitarian expedient. They say that these gods have a human form and even resemble some of the other animals, and make other statements that derive from those already mentioned or are closely akin to them. Now, if we are to draw a distinction between these statements and accept only the first, namely, that they thought that the primary essences are gods, we must regard this as being a divinely inspired saying. Since, in all probability, every craft and philosophy has been repeatedly re-discovered and perfected only to be destroyed again, so too these opinions of theirs have been preserved to this day but only in a residual way. To this extent only, then, are the opinions of our forefathers and the primordial tradition intelligible to us.[50]

Aristotle, then, lends his authority to the now unfashionable theory of Wilhelm Schmidt, who held that religion starts as an exalted monotheism and is then reduced to a more or less puerile polytheism to accord with the tastes of the common people: it is in constant need of reform. The history of Christianity and Islam shows that there is much truth in what he says. Not only do other gods (in this case deified saints) appear beside the true God, but religion itself becomes a department of state, though retaining its priestly status.[51] All this must have been repugnant to the truly religious man, just as state interference in Church affairs is resented by serious-minded Anglicans today. As a force working towards social cohesion, however, it is invaluable, and the priesthood offers a comfortable retirement to elderly gentlemen who are no longer capable of sustained work. And so, Aristotle sensibly says, 'the priesthood should not be manned by farmers or craftsmen since the gods should receive honour only from full citizens; and since the citizen body is divided into two halves, the military and the civil service, and since it is right and proper that all such as have retired on account of old age should render due service to the gods and spend their retirement in attending to their affairs, it is these who should be put in charge of religious affairs.'[52] If one doesn't take the state religion very seriously, this seems a very sensible arrangement, just as today it seems perfectly natural to make retired ambassadors vice-chancellors of universities or heads of Oxford or Cambridge colleges. Indeed, it would appear to be more sensible since the harm a temple priest can do is minimal in comparison with the potential for damage with which vice-chancellors and heads of colleges are invested.

Aristotle's attitude to the established religion is, then, one of benevolent tolerance, since it preserves a remnant of the truth about God which is the immemorial heritage of mankind. In addition, Aristotle seems to imply that, since he sanctions reverent service even to false gods, he must, by that token alone, approve of the same service to the true God. This service in fact takes the form of contemplation, as we shall see.

For Aristotle the true God must be beyond space and time, eternal, and wholly sufficient unto himself. In the twelfth book of the *Metaphysics* he is called the 'Unmoved Mover' and the 'thinking of thinking' or 'consciousness of consciousness'. He is, then, wholly transcendent and does not apparently concern himself with man. But this is not the whole story since the whole of Nature is permeated with the divine,[53] and this divine quality is pre-eminently present in man through his possession of Mind (*nous*) which sets him apart from all the other animals.

In considering Aristotle's God let us follow the method he himself would probably have followed, start with the individual and concrete, and proceed from there to the God of the Philosopher who emerges into the full light of day in the twelfth book of the *Metaphysics*. The region proper to the divine within the universe is, as we have seen, the heavenly spheres beyond the moon. In our own sublunar world (if we are to forget for the moment the divinity Aristotle attributes to bees)[54] the divine, though vaguely suffused throughout Nature, is present mainly in man 'who is the only one of the animals known to us who participates in the divine, or, if there are others, his share is the greatest.[55] With man, then, let us begin.

Like the other animals man is primarily a 'pairing' animal,[56] that is to say he reproduces himself by sexual intercourse. The first object of our inquiry must then be to try to discover how the divine principle in man is transmitted in the sexual act. Before we discuss this, however, we must say something about the Aristotelian concept of matter and form.

In real life there is no such thing as primary matter, for it is impossible for it to exist without some kind of 'form'. It is the totally indefinite, and as such has the potentiality of receiving an infinite number of forms.[57] In fact it *is* potentiality, that is to say, though being strictly no thing itself, it is that which is capable of developing into anything by receiving the impress of any of the innumerable forms that may alight on it. In a crucial passage[58] Aristotle makes a clear distinction between matter and pure nothingness (*sterēsis*, usually translated as 'privation', which, however, seems misleading here). 'We maintain', he says, 'that matter and pure nothingness are distinct, the first, namely, matter, being non-existent incidentally (since it has the potentiality both of being anything and of not being anything at all), whereas pure nothingness is non-existence of its very nature. Matter is very nearly and in a sense actually *is* a "being-ness" (*ousia*, 'substance'), which is totally out of the question in the case of pure nothingness.'

Matter, then, is pure potentiality waiting to receive form which is what makes a thing what it is. In this world, according to ancient Greek (and Indian) theory, the simplest forms imposed upon matter are the four elements – fire, air, water, and earth – which in their turn are composed of a combination of the four primary qualities which are the basic pairs of opposites – the hot and the cold, the moist and the dry. All things, then, are composed of matter which, in its pure state, is akin to nothingness, but which is for that very reason the *locus* of change through which one or other of the pairs of opposites plus the form that any particular piece of matter may assume, are 'actualised', that is to say come to exist as a concrete 'something'. Thus fire, for instance, is primary matter plus the primary qualities of the hot and the dry plus the 'form' of fire. The 'form' of fire, however, cannot exist on its own: it merely makes fire what it is – fieriness. In our world, however, fieriness does not exist apart from individual fires. Hence it will be the matter of any given fire that will distinguish it from all others. In the case of an individual, concrete fire the secondary matter may be anything combustible, but it will become an 'actual' fire only when the 'form' of fire has been impressed upon it by the substitution of one opposite – in this case the cold – by the other – the hot.

This, then, is Aristotle's answer to Parmenides. Though it is true that in God and in all divine existences there is no change because there is neither time nor space in which change as we understand it could take place, in our world this is made possible by the existence of matter, which is that in which all change takes place and through which change *can* take place.

Primary matter, as we have seen, cannot exist on its own, but the simplest forms of matter – the four elements – can and do; and these in turn serve as matter for higher and more complicated forms, which in their turn serve as matter for still higher forms. To take a very simple example – a table. Its matter is wood, its form 'table-ness'. It is *this* table as distinct from *that* table because the matter of which it is composed is different. Its 'material cause', that is to say the particular type of matter of which it is made, is wood; its 'efficient cause', that is the agency responsible for the change the wood undergoes, is the carpenter; its 'formal cause', that is to say what gives it the form of a table rather than a chair, is its 'form' – tableness; while its 'final cause', that is to say its *telos*, its 'end' and purpose and 'entelechy' – what it is when fully realised or 'actualised', to use the usual translation – and its *ti ēn einai*, its 'What was it to be?' is *this* fully actualised and reasonably perfect table which has received the form of the particular table the carpenter had in mind.

That the transformation of a given quantity of wood into a table could take place at all is due to the existence of matter, for matter is the potentiality for change. Of course there is always the possibility, indeed the probability, that the fully realised and actualised table will be defective and not a perfect copy of the blue-print of the table the carpenter had in mind, because, as we have seen, not only are all craftsmen liable to make mistakes but Nature herself is too. But this is the price we pay for being in the material world – a world in which mistakes or 'sins' are part and parcel of an existence that is subject to perpetual change.

As so often, we find the basic ideas of Greek philosophy expressed in primitive form in the Upanishads in India. There is a myth in the *Brihadāranyaka* Upanishad (1.2.1) which seems tailored to fit the key Aristotelian concept of matter and form. Like most myths it seems crude enough, but the idea behind it suddenly takes on a new significance in the light of Aristotle's philosophy. This is how it runs:

'In the beginning nothing at all existed here. This was enveloped by Death – by Hunger. For what is death but hunger? And Death bethought himself: "Would that I had a self." He roamed around offering praise; and from him, as he offered praise, water was born.'

This, you might say, is the concept of matter and form expressed in a mythological setting. In Aristotle, as we have seen, there is a distinction between matter which is 'no thing' though capable of receiving any and every form or none at all, and *sterēsis*, which, in an absolute sense, I have translated as 'pure nothingness', that is the total lack and negation of *any* form and therefore of Being itself which is the essence of all forms. In a relative sense it means a similar lack or negation of its opposite, as, for instance, the cold is the total lack and negation of the hot, the 'not-being' of the 'being-ness' of its opposite.[59]

This concept is totally distinct from that of matter. *Sterēsis* is pure negation and, as such, the total lack of all being *or becoming*; it is non-existence in an absolute sense, lack of all being whether actual or potential. Matter, on the other hand, is not-being in the sense that it cannot exist actually without form of some kind, but a kind of 'beingness' (*ousia*) in that it comes to be once it has received form. The fact that Aristotle called matter 'wood' (*hulē*) shows that he regarded it as something positive, something capable of a vast variety of transformations. In the case of an oak, for instance, it 'comes to be' in the shape of an acorn, grows, and, by growing, is slowly transformed into a tree – it changes in respect of both its quality and size (its 'What sort of?' and its 'How much or how many?', as Aristotle puts it in his far more concrete way). Finally it reaches its 'end', its consummation, its 'entelechy', its 'What was it to be?': a fulfilled and perfected tree, single and unique. Having reached its fulfilment it may be cut down and chopped up. As a tree it passes away and is 'negated', thereby being deprived of its own particular form – its 'tree-ness'. But it does not pass away absolutely, since it now becomes a higher sort of matter – tables, chairs, bookcases, houses, churches, gibbets, not to mention the Cross – each one of which has its own very different end and fulfilment. In all these transformations the secondary matter remains as a *hupokeimenon* – a 'substratum', or (in English) 'that which underlies' all these transformations. If, however, the table is burnt down, its form both as table and as wood is destroyed and negated, though matter of some sort persists (as ashes and smoke). This is its *sterēsis*: as wood it has been totally negated and *is not*.

Bearing all this in mind it will be seen that the 'nothing at all' of the Upanishad is Aristotelian matter, not pure nothingness; for besides being 'nothing at all', it is 'this', by which is meant the whole universe in a state of pure flux and lacking all definition; in this sense it is infinite because indefinite. Though it is described as 'death', it is death conceived of as 'hunger', a gaping void yearning to be filled. It has no 'self', no Aristotelian form, though it yearns to have one. The same myth appears, though couched in philosophical terms, in Aristotle's *Physics* (192 a16–23):

Granted that something divine, good, and desirable does exist, we admit that [there are two principles other than 'form' (which partakes of the divine), namely, matter and *sterēsis*, that is, the total or partial lack of one pole of any given pair of opposites], one of which is contrary to the [divine], while the other [matter] is, in accordance with its own nature, inclined to desire and yearn for it. . . . Now form cannot desire itself, since it is not defective; nor can either of the opposites[60] [desire it], for opposites are mutually destructive. The truth is that what desires form is matter, as the female desires the male, and the ugly the beautiful.

In this age of Women's Lib., it may seem strange that the desire that matter is alleged to have for form is compared to the desire that the female has for the male, since, contrary to all ancient traditions, the moderns tend to regard the male as being the more concupiscent of the two. Be that as it may, Aristotle, along with all the ancients, regarded the female as being inferior to the male, especially biologically, since, in his opinion, she appears to be a 'deformed male'.[61] In the act of procreation, however, it is the female who supplies the matter (though this is, of course, a very highly developed form of matter quite different from the barely existent primary matter we have been discussing), while the male supplies the form. Matter, indeed, 'which underlies [everything] is a cause which complements form in all things that come to be: [in this respect] it is just like a mother.'[62] In the sexual act itself 'it is the male who supplies the principle of movement and generation, the female who supplies the matter.'[63]

Now, since the soul is the 'form' of the body, it would seem that the soul is provided by the male parent, the body by the female. The soul is also the principle of life – 'that by which we live'[64] – and in this sense the matter provided by the mother is as important as the form supplied by the father, for in our world there can be no life apart from matter. This at least applies to the lower forms of soul, for soul is not an absolute unity, but there are grades of it corresponding to the major 'qualitative leaps' that can be discerned in the evolutionary process; for we share life not only with the other animals but also with the plants. Plants, however, participate in soul in the most rudimentary manner: their life consists of coming to be, growing by the absorption of nourishment from the immediate environment, withering, and finally passing away as individuals, but, by depositing their seeds in the ground, assuring that the species continues. (The word for 'species' in Greek, it should be noted, is the same as the word for 'form'.)

Animals, in addition to the nutritive faculty which alone is the 'soul' of plants, also possess the faculty of moving from place to place and that of perception. Like the plants too they reproduce themselves by the union of the sexes (for Aristotle was well aware that there was something akin to sexual reproduction among the plants). This again assures the survival of the species. And in this perpetual renovation of all living things on earth Aristotle saw an imitation in this imperfect world of the perfect, regular, and eternal circular motion of the heavenly bodies above, each of which was propelled by its own 'unmoved mover', while these in their turn were sustained by the Prime Unmoved Mover, who is God.

When we pass from the other animals to man, a totally new and divine element appears in the soul; and this is *Nous*, 'Mind, intellect, consciousness, self-awareness,' or simply 'awareness', for all these are possible translations. This alone is divine in man, and, if divine, then eternal and immortal. Yet in one passage Aristotle approves of those philosophers who say that 'the soul cannot exist without the body'.[65] If this is so, how can it survive the body?

At the beginning of his discussion on the soul Aristotle does not seem to have made up his mind whether Nous can survive without the body or not, and, if so, in what sense. 'About Nous and the contemplative faculty', he says, 'nothing is yet clear, but it may well be that there is a distinct kind of soul, and that that alone admits of being separated from the body, and thereby from matter in general, just as the eternal is distinct from the perishable.'[66] That this is so and how it is so he discusses later in his treatise *On the Soul* in a maddeningly ambiguous passage from which Aquinas developed his whole theory of 'active' and 'passive' intellect.

The soul also corresponds in a way to the end and purpose of man-made tools, and the 'end' is, of course, its 'form' which makes it what it is. Thus the soul 'is a substance ['being-ness'] corresponding to its own rationale [*logos*]. And this is the "What was it to be?" of any such body. Now, suppose that a tool – say, an axe – were a natural [living] body, then its "being-ness" would be what [it means] to *be* an axe, and this would be its soul. If, however, you were to separate this ['*being* an axe', that is if you were to deprive it of its proper function by damaging it], it would no longer *be* an axe, except that it still retains the same name. . . . However, it is not of this kind of [inanimate] body that the soul is the "What was it to be?" and its rationale, but rather of that kind of natural [living] body which has within itself a source of movement and rest.'[67] In other words, just as an axe ceases to be an 'actual', real axe once it is irrevocably damaged or worn out, so does a man cease to be a man once his soul is separated from his body. At death the matter of the body will dissolve into new types of matter, and these will be united with new forms, such as worms and thistles. His form too, apart from the Nous, will also cease to exist as a real, actual, and active entity (for all these meanings are present in the Greek word *energeia*, usually translated as 'actuality' as opposed to *dunamis* – unactualised, unrealised 'potentiality').

Leaving aside for the moment the apparently mysterious phrase, the 'What was it to be?', we must now pass on to the equally mysterious problem of how Nous – self-consciousness, intellect, Mind – which is divine, can be present in man at all.

We have seen that, according to Aristotle, in the act of love the male parent supplies the 'form', the female the 'matter'. Nous, then, must somehow be present in the male sperm, potentially at least, if not actually, or it must have been injected from outside; and, if so injected, with which part of the soul will it be associated?

Now in a celebrated passage in his treatise *On the Soul* (430 a) Aristotle makes a distinction between the *poiētikos* Nous (the active, 'creative' Nous) and the *pathētikos* Nous (the 'passive' Nous), which we shall shortly have to consider. Of the two only the active, creative one is immortal, since the passive Nous must die along with the body. If this is 'actually' so at the time of death, it would seem that it must have been potentially so at the moment of conception. The evidence of Aristotle's remarkable treatise *On the Generation of Animals* fully supports this theory; for there we read: 'We are, then, left with the conclusion that Nous alone enters in *from outside* as an additional factor, and that it alone is divine; for bodily activity has nothing whatever to do with the activity of Nous.'[68]

This, however, would seem to be overstating the case, since so long as bodily life lasts, the creative Nous *does* operate through the passive Nous, which, since it dies along with the other faculties of the soul, necessarily retains some link with the body and, through the body's senses, with the world. In fact precisely the same connection seems to exist within the male sperm. And so Aristotle goes on to say that semen in general contains a hot substance which makes individual spermatozoa fertile. This he describes as a 'breath' or 'spirit' (*pneuma*) 'which is enclosed within the sperm and within the "foam-like" stuff [with which the sperm is associated]'; and this, he says, 'is analogous to the element which is proper to the stars'. This element the Greeks called *aither*; and it was within this element that the gods of popular belief as well as the heavenly bodies lived and moved and had their being. The motion of the stars is swift, utterly uniform, and circular, and the ether (*aithēr*) is so called because 'it is always on the run [*aei thein*] throughout eternal time'.[69]

This 'ether' is, of course, not God, but it is divine in the sense that it is coherent and continuous and the *locus* of circular movement which is divine because of its utter simplicity. That this divine *milieu* should be composed of the 'foam-like' stuff that is supposed to be present in semen may seem bizarre; but it is less so if you consider that, apart from God who is totally sufficient unto himself, all beings, whether human or divine, must have their proper sphere of activity: the ether for the heavenly bodies beyond our own sublunar world; the 'passive' Nous for the divinely active Nous in man; the whole soul for the whole Nous which is its highest part; the body for the soul; and lastly this 'foam-like' stuff which is receptive of the Nous 'that comes from outside' for the semen.

The source of this strange idea is mythological, as Aristotle himself tells us. 'It would seem', he says, 'that even the ancients were not unaware of the fact that the true nature of semen was like foam, since they called the supreme goddess of sexual intercourse (Aphrodite) by its name [*aphros*].'[70]

The legend is told by Hesiod in his *Theogony* (189–90). After 'crooked-minded' Kronos had castrated his father Uranus, the primeval sky-god, and thrown his severed phallus behind his back, 'no sooner had he cut off his phallus with flint and cast it from the dry land into the surging sea than the ocean bore it away for a long, long time. Then a white foam from the immortal flesh rose up around it, and in it a young girl received nourishment [and grew]. First she drew near to god-haunted Cythera, then she went from there to sea-girt Cyprus. Then did she emerge as a venerable, lovely goddess. . . . And so both gods and men call her Aphrodite for that she was nourished in the foam.'

The legend was, of course, well known to Aristotle as it would have been to any free-born Greek, who probably learnt it in the nursery. It is his use of it that is intriguing. The 'foam-like' stuff is the seed of Uranus, the heavenly Father. It is therefore pre-eminently divine; and it is this divine seed which is also akin to the heavenly 'ether' which we male persons are privileged to bear within us. Of its own nature the seed is instinct with desire, and it is therefore impelled to find the 'matter' appropriate to itself. In the ancient legend the 'matter' was the watery ocean (an essentially feminine symbol according to C. G. Jung and his disciples) in which the seed was nurtured until it emerged as a new creature, the 'venerable and lovely' goddess of love.

The male semen, then, which contains the 'form' of a new being potentially, actualises it by mingling with the female ovum in the womb; and the newly actualised being will necessarily be one driven on by desire, since this is what the 'foam-born' Aphrodite is. But since Nous, the eternal and unchanging, had been inserted into the seminal foam, man is potentially both Aphrodite *and* Nous: he is animated by both desire and reason; but by far the greater of the two is reason – Nous, for it is this alone that separates him from the other animals and makes him divine – but not yet divine in actual fact, but only potentially so. But since Nous, being divine, must be more honourable than desire and prior to it in the scale of value, man's end and fulfilment – his entelechy and full actualisation – must be to realise himself as Nous. And this he can only do through desire itself, *if rightly directed*.

Now I think we are in a position to ask what Aristotle really meant by that curious phrase, the 'What was it to be?' Let us put it in the form of a catechism:

Q. What were you before you were conceived in your mother's womb?

A. Nothing at all, or very nearly so.

Q. Can you be a little more precise?

A. Yes. There was a certain grade of matter in my mother's womb which yearned for the form my father was to provide.

Q. What sort of thing was this form which was present in your father's seed?

A. The form inherent in the seed was the foam (*aphros*) of love (Aphrodite).

Q. Was there nothing else present in your father's seed?

A. No. But something was injected into it from outside.

Q. What was that?

A. Some kind of divine breath or spirit deriving from the ether which is the eternal, self-coherent element in and through which the gods live and in which they rejoice. (Aside) I am not sure I really understand that.

Q. What was the form of that spirit?

A. Nous: creative Mind, creative self-consciousness, but still only potential in that it needed the matter in my mother's womb in order to become a real, actual, active, individual member of the species *homo sapiens.*

Q. What happened when your father and mother came together?

A. The form of love and the form of Mind were impressed on to the matter in my mother's womb.

Q. And what came to be out of this?

A. A new human being, having all the potentialities that are wide open to all human beings, for wisdom and for folly, for good and for evil, for love, for indifference, for hate.

Q. So *you* came to be as yourself and no one else. But *what were you to be*?

A. What I was to be is what I *am* in eternity – a creative Mind.

Q. But if this creative Mind is eternal and wholly self-sufficient, what need has it to display itself as *you* who are anything but self-sufficient?

A. It had no need. But since it is creative and of its very nature active, it must have *wanted* to create a new life in time, just as a painter wants to paint a picture so as to objectify and actualise what is already real and actual in his mind. He wants to contemplate in time what he *is* in eternity.

Q. What, then, is your end and fulfilment?

A. In ordinary language my end is, of course, death. But my true End – what those silly Latins call my 'final cause' – is to have painted the picture of my life in as perfect a way as in me lies. This should have been achieved when I am forty-nine.[71] If not, then I shall have failed in my purpose:

I shall not have become fully 'what I was to be'. My creative Mind will have painted a bad picture: it will have failed, gone badly astray, 'sinned', as the English Christians so oddly translate our *hamartanein* which really means little more than getting things wrong.

Here endeth the catechism.

The true essence of man is, then, his Nous, or, more strictly, his *poiētikos* Nous, his creative, craftsman, 'poetic' Mind, which makes his life, contemplates the life he has made, and then, if he has deliberately chosen and acquired what is noblest and best and most in accord with reason in this world, will 'make, create, and produce (*poiēsei*) the contemplative vision of God'.[72]

The Hindus teach that there are three ends to be pursued in human life: *dharma*, *artha*, and *kāma*. Roughly these may be translated as 'justice', 'self-interest', and 'desire'. Desire, of course, implies its satisfaction and therefore includes pleasure. Of these three ends *dharma* is the most excellent, *artha* less so, and pleasure least of all. The balanced man, however, will try to combine the three. Aristotle too makes the same distinction. Decent men should pursue the noble (*kalon*), self-interest, and pleasure.[73] It is the noble, however, more often called *aretē* – 'excellence', and particularly moral excellence – that is the only source of true happiness; and since happiness or beatitude (it is difficult to find the right word to translate the Greek *eudaimonia*) is not possible without pleasure, it must also include the highest pleasure. And this can only be found in what is highest in man – what makes him higher than the other animals and only a little lower than God: and that is his Nous, more specifically his 'creative, craftsman, poetic' Nous, the eternal which contemplates the Eternal.

As in Hinduism, then, moral excellence is accompanied by a pleasure far more intense than the animal pleasures of the flesh and the vulgar human pleasure of self-aggrandisement, for it leads on to the supreme pleasure of contemplation. But moral excellence is not possible without right *knowledge*: you cannot be happy unless you know what is really good for you, not simply what seems to be so. And this may have to be learnt the hard way. For, as the *Bhagavad-Gītā* (18. 37–8) says: that pleasure 'which a man enjoys after much effort spent, making an end thereby of suffering, which at first seems like poison but in time transmutes itself into what seems to be ambrosia, is called pleasure through excellence, for it springs from that serenity which comes from apperception of the self.'

That Aristotle too had his own ideas about 'apperception of the self' we shall soon see. As to the difficulties on the road, he too had no illusions; for he knew that 'great and repeated misfortunes can crush and soil this blessed state both by the pain they cause and by the hindrance they offer to many [laudable] activities. Yet even in adversity nobility shines through, when a man endures repeated and severe misfortunes, taking them in his stride, not because he does not feel the pain, but because he is a thoroughbred and has greatness of soul.'[74] In this Aristotle aligns himself with the Christians rather than with the early Buddhists and the Hindu yogis: you must endure suffering with serenity and dignity, you should not immunise yourself against it by transcending it.

Aristotle makes a clear distinction between the active and the contemplative lives and comes down on the side of the latter. This may be so absolutely in a perfect world, but in practice it can only apply to older men since the young are by nature sensual, quick to change their minds, impulsive, ambitious, though good-natured, open, starry-eyed in their hope of better things to come.[75] The mere fact that Aristotle devoted almost the whole of both his ethical treatises to the pursuit of active excellence in the world and only a small portion of the last book to the contemplative life would seem to indicate that he came to experience contemplation rather late in life, perhaps at the age of forty-nine which he considers to be the age at which man reaches his full mental stature.[76] If this were not so, it would be difficult to see why he picks on so precise a figure as forty-nine. Why not settle for the obvious round number fifty?

The Greek word *theōria* has several meanings. Basically, it means 'sight' and is in fact used to mean what we would call a 'show', our own word 'theatre' being derived from the same root.[77] Secondly it can mean what its English derivative 'theory' means, and thirdly the contemplation of things divine and the vision of God 'made' or 'produced' by the creative Mind.[78] It is in this last sense that *theōria* is contrasted with the active life; for contemplation is a leisure occupation and is not easily combined with menial work, as Martha querulously realised, only to be told by Jesus that Mary who did nothing but contemplate him, nothing but gaze at him, 'had chosen the better part'.[79] So too Aristotle tells us that 'leisure is the end and purpose of business'[80] and that true beatitude is only to be found in it rather than in just getting things done.[81]

In both the active and contemplative lives the mind is necessarily operative, but more directly so in the latter. For the primary function of mind is to construct 'theories' without, however, allowing them to prevail over any new facts that may emerge after any particular theory has been formulated.[82] Secondly – and more importantly – Mind is concerned with pure contemplation in which all distinction between knower and known seems to melt away. None of this, however, involves the 'creative' mind directly; rather, it is the province of the 'passive' mind. For in the process of contemplation the passive mind begins to operate in a sphere in which matter no longer exists but in which lower 'forms' serve as matter to higher ones until the stage is reached when knower and known seem to be all one in a single act of knowing,[83] the soul thus 'becoming in a sense all things that *are*' – the pantheist's vision of actually *being* all things, which seems so strange to us but perfectly natural and almost a matter of course to the authors of the Upanishads.

By direct experience[84] Aristotle knew very well what the pantheists were talking about, but as a scientist, a rationalist, and a philosopher he knew that when people make such extravagant claims as to *be* 'a season, the son of seasons, arisen from the womb of space, seed of brilliance, glory of the year, the Self of every single being', as the author of the *Kaushītaki* Upanishad (1.6) does, they are talking nonsense. What they meant was that the *form* of all these material objects was experienced internally. It is idiotic to say that you are actually identical with a stone, but it is anything but idiotic to say that the *form* of the stone is in your soul.[85]

The passive mind, or, to transliterate the actual Greek word used, the 'pathetic' mind, having *seen* that all things are one and present within itself, very naturally has a severe attack of megalomania and asks itself the rhetorical question: 'When all has become one's very Self, then with what should one see whom?'[86] For in very truth it has 'become the All'.[87] But poor passive mind, 'pathetic' as he is, is in for a rude shock. He, the omniscient and therefore omnipotent thinker, who has *seen* his identity with the whole universe, now has a very unnerving experience: he is slipping out of the whole world in which matter plays its due part and with every aspect of which he has identified himself, and has entered into the 'divine' sphere where he himself has become an object of thought. The pantheistic vision in which 'All is One and One is All' fades, and although he *has* become the whole universe in a sense, he is calmly informed by his superior and 'maker' the 'creative, craftsman' Mind that in the eyes of the divine world he is what matter is in the phenomenal world – nothing, or very nearly so – since he too, like the body and the purely animal soul which animates it, must die. Even if it were true that he *is* the whole universe, the universe itself is one vast machine of coming to be and passing away, of death and resurrection endlessly repeated but in no wise eternal and unmoved. What creative Mind tells him is this:

Since there is in the whole of Nature something which serves as matter to every kind of thing (*and it is that which is potentially all of them*), while on the other hand there is something else which is their cause and, as it were, their 'maker' [*poiētikon*] insofar as it 'makes' all things – rather like a craft or profession in relation to the matter [which is proper to itself] – it necessarily follows that these differences must exist in the soul too. So there is one kind of mind which is capable of *becoming* all things, and another which will be able to *make* all things (for this will be its inherent disposition, as you might say), just as light [makes all colours]. For in a certain way light 'makes' colours which were potential only into actual colours. *This* [creative] Mind is something quite separate: it cannot be affected by anything, nor is it mixed with anything, for its essence is pure actuality, pure activity, pure energy.[88]

Now that which makes is always more honourable than that which submits to the making, just as the first principle is more honourable than matter . . . . But there can be no question of its thinking at one time and not at another. It is separate, just what it is; and this alone is deathless and eternal. But we cannot normally bring it up into consciousness, for it cannot be affected by anything. But the passive mind – the mind which can be so affected – *is* perishable: and without the creative Mind it cannot think of anything at all.[89]

So here it is, once again with us, the Nous-Mind which entered Aphrodite's 'foam' 'from outside', now seen as bidding farewell to Aphrodite's world of matter-and-form with its poor, passive, pathetic, female mind which thinks it is the One and the All, but which dies and will always die because the goddess of animal love which gave it birth must in the end slay it, for this is the inexorable rule of all *living* things on earth. Sexual orgasm is not only the prelude to a new life: it is also the death of two egos in something greater than either. This might be explained as the work of the 'innate spirit', that divine presence which, according to Aristotle, accompanies the seed of the male.

God, then, is immanent in a generalised form throughout Nature, but especially present, at least potentially, in the 'innate' (more accurately 'con-nate', 'with-born', *sumphuton*) spirit infused into the semen before conception and then fully actualised, realised, and brought into the full light of consciousness in the creative Mind which will return to its eternal home at death. This Mind, which alone survives death, is a *separate* essence and therefore has no recollection of the passive mind and the life it had created through it on earth. It is now free, 'separate, a thing alone . . . deathless and eternal'. If it is all this, then is it not identical with God himself, the Unmoved Mover, who is also the 'thinking of thinking' and thereby the 'Creative Mind' *par excellence*?

The answer is 'No': it is 'divine and godlike', but it is not God. 'What we are investigating is this,' says Aristotle, ' "What is the principle of motion in the soul?" ' The answer is clear enough. Just as in the universe out there God causes everything to move, so does the divine in us cause everything to move in some sense. But the source of reason (*logos*) is not reason itself but something higher. What, then, could be higher than understanding and Mind except God?[90]

Our creative Mind, then, is that divine spark already inherent, though only potentially so, in the male sperm, fully actualised and realised at the height of contemplation. In these rare moments we are like God in that we realise that our true 'self', as the Hindus would say, is eternal and unmoving, yet at the same time directs and controls the movement of the other faculties of the soul and body, just as God controls the whole universe as a general controls his army.[91]

The soul, while still in the body, is divided into two parts: Nous on the one hand and desire or 'yearning' on the other. It is the function of Nous to control desire and to see that it is guided in the right direction. If it fails to do so, a disequilibrium results, an unnatural state of affairs which Aristotle calls *hamartia*, a 'mistake', which English-speaking Christians have chosen to translate as 'sin'. Desire is, of course, an essential element in love of any kind, particularly sexual love. It seems strange, then, that Aristotle should use the words 'yearning' and 'passionate love' when he speaks of man's relationship to God.[92] But perhaps this is not really so, for it is of the very nature of creatures bounded by space and time to strive to get what is good for them. The trouble is that most of them do not know what this is; and so it is the business of Mind to guide desire to what it really wants though it may not know what this is. Now, what it really wants is to be wholly and absolutely independent from space and time, and wholly sufficient unto itself. But man is not like this, and so he must be content to desire Him who alone truly *is*, that is, God. This desire, then, must be diverted from transient things and directed to the Unmoved, eternal One.[93] This may not be easy, but once desire finds its true goal it falls passionately in love with the Unmoved One and thereby, in some sense, causes him to move, that is to say it causes him to act on it as a magnet acts on a piece of iron. For God, it should be remembered, is pure *energeia*, pure actuality, activity, *and* energy. He is not merely at rest (for rest is no more than an absence of motion), but even more than the heavenly 'ether' he 'is always on the run'. Though Unmoved, he might be said to move with an infinite velocity, which, insofar as we can understand these things at all, would be equivalent to not moving at all, just as a torch whirled round at great speed looks like one continuous circle of light.

Matter longs for form as the female longs for the male, since the male contains the divine 'innate spirit' in his semen. It is, then, only reasonable to suppose that 'form' itself in the shape of the creative Mind, which is itself the 'form of forms' in the human soul[94] must yearn for and passionately love the universal 'Form of forms' which is God. In other words the creative Mind, which is itself divine, must play the woman to the infinitely attractive male who is God. This relationship between the soul and God is a commonplace in all theistic mystical literature, whether Christian, Muslim, or Hindu. In your relationship to God you 'become a woman', as Meister Eckhardt[95] said. This seems to be clearly implied by the use of the words for yearning (*oregomai*) and passionate love (*erō*) and not the ordinary word for love (*philō*) which can be used for every kind of love from purely carnal passion to the love that the contemplative has for his companion whom he regards as his second self.

It would appear, then, that when the creative Mind turns its back on the world, which it must do at death and can do in moments of enlightenment, that is of complete spiritual awareness (and, it should be remembered, to be a Buddha means to be 'aware and awake'), then it '*makes* the contemplation of God'.[96] This is, however, the last thing it 'makes', for its relationship to God is one in which it remains passive while God takes the active part as its benefactor. In this respect it is a relationship of total dependence, more like the relationship of son to father; for 'the relationship of father to son is the same as that of God to man, and the one who does good to the one who has good done to him, and, more generally, of every natural ruler to every natural subject'.[97] Hence the relationship of God to the universe at large is compared to the relationship of a general to his army; and, since an army is composed of disciplined soldiers holding different ranks, it seems reasonable to suppose that these soldiers are the 'creative Minds' that were once associated with individual passive minds, souls, and bodies in this life. And so, Aristotle says:

We must consider too in which way the nature of the Whole possesses the good and the superlatively good; whether as something separate and [existing as] itself by itself, or as order, or again in both senses, as is the case of an army. For its well [-being] is both *in* the order and *is* the general. But it consists principally in the general; for the general is not dependent on the order, but the order depends on him. All things, indeed, are ordered together in some way, but not all alike.[98]

Now it is usually assumed that Aristotle's Unmoved Mover,

who is also the 'thinking of thinking', must necessarily be indifferent to the world and to man in particular. This is plainly not so, as the simile of the general and the army shows. It is quite true that he says that 'it would be ridiculous to complain about God not returning our love in the same way that we love him, or for a subject to make the same complaint about his sovereign; for it is the part of the [ideal] ruler to be loved, not to love, or to love in a different way. And the pleasure [in loving and being loved] differs too: for the pleasure a man who is self-sufficient finds in his property or son is not one and the same as the pleasure a man who lacks both, feels on acquiring either of them.'[99]

God's love for his creatures, then, is that of a sovereign for his subject or of a benefactor for his beneficiary; and of the two, according to Aristotle, it is the ruler and the benefactor who has the greater love. 'Benefactors', he says, 'seem to love those on whom they confer benefits more than the beneficiary loves the benefactor. And since this seems contrary to reason, we ask why this should be so.'[100] To compare this relationship to that of a creditor to a debtor is rather superficial, since the creditor has an interest in his debt being repaid whereas the true benefactor has no such ulterior motive. For 'the man who does good loves and feels affection for (*agapō*) those who are done good to, even if he is not going to get anything out of them and is never likely to do so.'[101] The relationship between the two is exactly the same as that between the creative Mind (the Mind that 'does something to' someone or 'makes' something (*poiei*) and the passive mind which has something done to it or is made (*paskhei*). These two Greek words are used both of the relationship of a man to a woman and of a father to a son. In the one case the man 'does something to' the woman: in the other he 'makes' the son, just as a painter 'makes' a picture.

'The same thing happens to the artist,' Aristotle says:

All artists feel more affection for their work than the work would feel for the artist, were it to come to life. Perhaps this is more particularly true of poets [*poiētas*] – 'makers' *par excellence* – for they feel an excessive affection for their poems, cherishing them as [parents cherish] their children. The position of the benefactor is just like this; for the person who has had good done to him is his own work. Hence the benefactor feels more affection for him than [the beneficiary who is his own] work will feel for his maker. The reason for this is that all things choose and love Being, for we exist actually simply by being alive and active. In a sense, then, he who has made something actually *is* the work he has made. He cherishes his work because he cherishes Being. This is wholly natural: for the work reveals as actually existent that which had [previously] only been potentially so.[102]

God, then, who is the supreme object of yearning and passionate love, is at the same time the general to whom all other things are subordinate; and, as such, being totally sufficient unto himself, he can return the kind of love that a ruler feels for his subject, father for son, poet for poem (which in Greek also means 'maker for what is made'). This seems to follow quite logically if we read the twelfth book of the *Metaphysics* concurrently with the last two books of both the *Nicomachean* and the *Eudemian Ethics* which discuss first friendship, then pleasure, and lastly contemplation.

Love, it would appear, is the missing link between the Unmoved Mover and the divine world on the one hand and the human world on the other. The divinisation of man is as much the cornerstone of Aristotle's teleology as it is of Teilhard de Chardin's: for the 'What was it to be?' of the whole universe must be God, seen as pure 'entelechy', pure fulfilment.[103] It is the function of the human mind – the creative mind working through the passive one – to redirect the soul's yearning and passionate love from imagined goods to the supremely Good, which is pure Being, pure Thought – the 'thinking of thinking',[104] which can equally well be translated as the 'knowing of knowing', the 'understanding of understanding' or the 'awareness of awareness' – and pure Pleasure or Joy. The first step in this process is to learn human love, and since to love another means to love him for his own sake because he is your 'second self',[105] you must learn how to love yourself first.

Self-love can, of course, mean one of two things. In popular speech it may mean no more than selfishness; but this is not only trivial but also imprecise, for the soul is made up of two basic components, the one rational, the other irrational. The irrational is yearning (*orexis*) or desire; the rational is Mind,[106] while sense perception seems to hold an intermediary position between the two.[107] Yearning or desire is clearly the source of love; and if one is to love oneself, this means that yearning must love Mind and obey its promptings as a good son obeys the wise commands of his father. Yet, though there may be two 'natures' in the soul, the 'person' is one:[108] and so 'being in agreement with himself, he yearns for the same things with all his soul and wills his own good, both real and apparent.'[109] This means that his is a fully integrated personality in which mind and desire, being wholly united, together yearn for 'another self' – a friend – in and through whom they can contemplate the ultimate Good.

But there is a difficulty here. If man's creative Mind is divine, then it might be expected to resemble God in all respects; and God is by definition wholly sufficient unto himself, needing nothing. This argument, however, falls to the ground once you realise that your friend really *is* another self to you.[110] And so, by 'loving your neighbour as yourself', you are simply loving your higher self in another body. By being at one with yourself *and* your friend you will have attained in some sense a double self-sufficiency; for, if the friends are equally excellent, they will each benefit the other and be benefited by the other; there will be a mutual give and take, a mutual 'doing to' and 'being done to' between them, the result of which will be a perfect equilibrium.

You desire and yearn for what is pleasurable: for love is impossible without pleasure, being motivated by pleasure; and pleasure in itself is a good thing, though like other good things it can be misdirected by an immature or perverse mind. Indeed it is possible that your yearnings and 'drives' may be intrinsically right and directed to the right object – not by Mind, but by a different kind of 'knowledge' (*gnōsis*) which has nothing to do with reason,[111] being directly inspired by God.[112] When this is so, your own rational judgement may be hopelessly at fault.[113]

Pleasure in itself is not evil, as Plato had suggested in the *Philebus*: like the world the good God made in the Book of Genesis it is good if for no other reason than that God himself, the Unmoved Mover and Understanding of Understanding, takes pleasure in himself: indeed he *is* pure, unadulterated Pleasure; for, as Aristotle roundly affirms, 'the absolutely good and the absolutely pleasurable are the same'.[114] It is not the desire for pleasure that is wrong because without pleasure there can be no happiness. The real 'sin' or mistake is committed by the mind in failing to exercise its rightful authority over desire.

The pleasure you derive from the love of another is greater than the pleasure you take in the integration of yourself because it is shared; and sharing is natural to man because he is a social animal. The Christian hermit and the Indian Sannyasin are deviations from the mean, and that is rarely, if ever, a good thing. Hence, Aristotle concludes (though with some hesitation) that the idea of self-sufficiency must be modified and broadened out into a fuller self-sufficiency which comprises like-minded friends whom you love because they are in a sense yourself: for 'it would perhaps be absurd to represent the truly blessed man as a hermit; for no man would choose to keep all good things for himself, since man is a social being, and it is natural for him to live with others'.[115]

Yet, however much your friend may be another self to you, so long as you are in this world, it is pointless to try to be anyone other than yourself through ecstasy ('standing outside yourself') or 'enthusiasm' ('being possessed by a god'), since you do not know what sort of 'god' or demon may choose to possess you. And so the good and serious man 'desires to live as himself and to be preserved for ever – and most of all that part of him which thinks. For to *be* is a "good" for the serious man, and everyone wishes good things for himself; and no one would choose to possess every possible good if that meant becoming someone else (for only God possesses the [whole] good *now*). Rather, he would be content to be whatever he happens to be. For it would seem that every man *is* what he thinks and knows, or at least predominantly so.'[116]

Unfortunately great-souled men are few and far between, and it is only with such that lasting friendship is possible. Hence no good and serious man can expect to have more than a very few worthwhile friends. If this is so, then contemplation can best be pursued in a small and tightly-knit community devoted to a life of moral excellence and refined pleasure; for this will bring you to the highest pleasure of all, which is identical with the 'superlatively Good', and in this all desire will fade away since it will have achieved fulfilment,[117] Such a compact society will be best adapted to a life of serene contemplation; and, just as a

balanced diet will not be over-seasoned with too many rich
sauces,[118] so will the contemplative life not be deluged with
too much 'engodded' ecstasy. Such a life, however, can only be
lived by a small group of friends who already love one another.
This may be asking a lot, for even in a small community nerves
tend to be frayed, whereas in a large one loving one's neighbour
as oneself can be 'one hell of a job' (*ergōdes*).[119]

It will be remembered that in the *Metaphysics* God is described
as being the object of passionate love, but, though it is nowhere
suggested that he is a 'jealous' God like his Hebrew counterpart,
the fact remains that for human beings it is rarely possible to be
in love with more than one person at the same time.[120] Hence,
when the creative Mind falls in love with God through the
yearning with which it is now indissolubly linked, it has no
choice but to turn its back on all transient things and, though
still bound by the ties of equal love to its chosen friends, to
devote itself to the divine love-affair by 'creating' or 'producing'
out of itself the 'contemplation of God'. And, just as in man the
creative Mind is both ruler and goal of the whole soul, so too, in
contemplation, God is seen not merely as a 'ruler in the sense
that he exercises command' (though he does that too as the general
in command of his universal army), 'but as that *for the sake of
which* wisdom (*phronēsis*) exercises command . . . for God lacks
nothing'. So 'it is contemplation which is superlatively good
and the noblest standard. And if any choice should intervene
that stands in the way of the service and contemplation of God
through either deficiency or excess, then that is worthless and
bad.'[121]

Contemplation is, of course, pre-eminently the concern of the
creative Mind, which, though it may from time to time transcend
reason, remains quintessentially rational. This is made abundantly
clear in the closing lines of the *Eudemian Ethics*[122] where we
read: 'This is the best possible standard for the soul, that it
should be as little conscious as possible of its own irrational part
as such.'

Even so, Aristotle admits that there is another type of
'knowledge' (*gnōsis*) which is quite different from discursive
thought (*epistēmē*)[123] and manifests itself in Platonic 'enthusiasm'
and ecstasy. This he appears to identify with something higher
than both discursive thought and Mind itself, and 'what can this

be but God?'[124] This plainly worried him, since what is higher than Mind can only be the 'thinking of thinking', the 'understanding of understanding', as he himself tells us in the *Metaphysics*. And yet, and yet . . . Aristotle had associated with Plato long enough to be very wary of this wholly irrational aspect of God. However, being Aristotle, he was too honest to disregard it; and he had to admit that, in some sense, this higher principle had an unaccountable and unpredictable side to its nature which manifests itself as 'chance', that is whatever it may be that produces such strange phenomena as prophecy and divine or demonic possession which cannot be explained in natural, 'physical' terms (nowadays we would say that they cannot be explained by science). These cannot be ascribed to Nature because Nature follows its own law; and these things follow no ascertainable law at all. More disturbingly, they happen to people not otherwise distinguished in any way. This was not to Aristotle's liking and he is therefore moved to say: 'It is surely incongruous that God or even a minor deity should choose people like this and not the best and most wise.'[125]

These manifestations *are*, however, inspired by a principle higher than discursive thought, and it *is* irrational. Aristotle calls it *hormē*, which can be translated as 'drive', 'thrust', 'hunch', or 'intuition'. Those who are favoured with this gift are called *eutuchēs* – 'lucky' or 'favoured by chance'; and the annoying thing is that 'they [actually] succeed in whatever their drive impels them to do though they are themselves devoid of reason. So they have no interest in deliberation, but they possess a principle of this sort which is higher than Mind and deliberation . . . and [this is] "enthusiasm"[126] – "possession by a god".' This possession must mean a mystical experience of what the Muslims call the 'drunken' variety. It is characteristic of these people that 'they *use* the divine; and this divine quality sees both the future and the present[127] – and sees them rightly; yet their reason is suspended. Hence manic-depressives, apart from their other qualities, also have "true" dreams. It would, then, seem that this principle [of chance] is more free to operate when reason is suspended, just as blind people have better memories than others because their ability to remember things seen is in a state of [permanent] suspension.'

Having considered these disturbing facts Aristotle concludes:

'And so it is clear that there are two types of spontaneous intuition [*eutuchia*, literally 'good fortune' or 'chance'], one of which is divine. Such a man seems to get things right through the agency of God (or a god) and he is liable to get them right because he follows his [divinely directed] drive. The other type, however, gets things right against [this divinely directed drive, presumably because he follows some kind of demonic drive]. Both, however, are irrational. The former kind of spontaneous intuition is more continuous and coherent: the latter is not continuous or coherent at all'.[128]

I have quoted this passage in full because, so far as I know, this is the only occasion on which Aristotle discusses the nature of 'enthusiasm' or 'divine possession', which is an *irrational* irruption of the supernatural into human affairs – the kind of irruption so horrifyingly depicted by Euripides in the *Bacchae* and the *Madness of Heracles* the kind that leads to ecstatic murder, a modern case of which is considered in Chapter 3 of this book. The point Aristotle is making – and rightly making – is that the mystical experience which is totally spontaneous and due only to chance or which 'uses the divine' as Yogis do, is not super-rational, as its practitioners would have us believe, but simply irrational. Ec-stasy, 'to get outside yourself', is contrary to Nature, a *hamartia* – a mistake – and a deviation from your final end, your 'What was it to be?', into self-dissolution and madness.

And yet 'enthusiasm' is not to be condemned out of hand. Just as tragedy purges the soul by inspiring us with the emotions of pity and terror,[128] so does sacred music inspire not only these but also 'enthusiasm' – a state of religious excitement, then, such as is induced by rhythmic singing and dancing, the result of which is ecstasy, the Shamanistic experience of 'being outside yourself'. This is salutary enough, since it is like taking a violent spiritual purge, a drastic method of clearing out your spiritual ordure. The 'catharsis' thus experienced will bring pleasurable relief.[130] So too, in watching a tragedy, if you are to derive the maximum benefit from it, you must be an ecstatic, you must get outside of yourself and identify yourself with the hero; and for this you will need a streak of madness.[131] No doubt 'enthusiasm' exists in all of us to some extent, but it must be kept under control since true contemplation means not to get outside of yourself but to experience and actualise and bring to the surface what is already in the heart of your being, your creative, 'poetic' Mind.

When you do realise the divine within yourself, you will have put all earthly things behind you, you will have witnessed and identified yourself with the actors in the human tragedy, you will have 'seen' the 'show', but now it is time to see the 'showing', as Julian of Norwich called the contemplation of God. As in the Sānkhya system in India there is nothing wrong with Nature, our world of space and time, but because it is transient it cannot house the absolute Good. But the absolute Good is also the Unmoved Mover who 'moves' us by inspiring us with passionate love. Under the influence of this terrific attraction we say goodbye to the stage of the world, fully content to have been seen by the contemplative Mind which the relevant Sanskrit text calls, appropriately enough from the Aristotelian point of view, *purusha* the 'male person'. He 'is like the spectator at a play: [Nature] brings the play to an end[132]. . . As a dancer stops dancing once she has shown herself to the audience, so does Nature stop once she has shown herself to *purusha*. In various ways Nature works for *purusha*'s sake, though he has no purpose at all, ministering to him though he does not minister to her, possessed of attributes though he has none himself. There is nothing more chivalrous than Nature, or so I think, for, content that she has been seen, she never again comes within the range of *purusha*'s sight.'[133]

And now it is time for us, through our creative minds, to gaze upon the motionless but pulsating form of the Unmoved Mover himself. He is, as we know, also the 'thinking of thinking', 'understanding of understanding', 'consciousness of consciousness', 'awareness of awareness' (the choice of translation at this stage is wide open); but he is also that without which no good can exist and which cannot be conceived of otherwise than as simple – 'the first principle on which the whole universe and all Nature depend. And his mode of being is like that superlatively good mode of being that we too can experience *for a short time*. But this is how he *always* is (though this is impossible for us), and his actuality, activity, and energy[134] are *pleasure*.'[135] To be for a few minutes at one with the divine Pleasure, the absolute Joy that God takes in himself, is all that Aristotle asked for. He didn't ask much, but what he asked for he got. And since in both his treatises on ethics he arrives at this absolute Pleasure through a minute analysis of every kind of love, it would seem reasonable to suppose that he saw this Pleasure in terms of perfect self-love first, and secondly in terms of an active love of all that is not yet perfect; for the pleasure of love is necessarily in the lover absolutely, since it is he who 'acts upon' the beloved, whereas the beloved is the passive recipient of his activity and actuality.[136] Since God is perfect, and 'acting on' is necessarily more excellent than 'to be acted on' just as to make is more excellent than to be made, it necessarily follows that he is not only the object of passionate love but also in some sense actively in love himself. If this is so, then Aristotle's God is not only pure, unmoved Being which is yet the source of all movement and change, not only the 'thinking of thinking', but also absolute Pleasure and absolute Joy – the lover, the beloved, and the love that unites them. He is the *Sat, Cit, Ānanda* – the Being, Thinking, Pleasure – of the Hindus and the Christian Trinity spelt out in intelligible terms.

As to the second member of this Trinity, the divine Nous: how are we to translate it here? For it seems to include what the *Eudemian Ethics* calls the 'greater than Nous'.[137] In my last book I translated it as 'awareness', and that is no doubt a possible translation; but now I think it is perhaps better to leave it in the Greek, bearing in mind the dreadful misunderstandings that have arisen in Christianity through translating the Greek *logos* as 'Word'. So let us follow Aristotle on his pilgrimage from his humble beginning as an 'innate spirit' incarnate in the foam-like semen to his magnificent end when he meets his 'What was Aristotle to be?' as he actually *is* for ever – Aristotle being in absolute Being, Aristotle thought by the 'Thinking of thought', Aristotle loved by absolute Joy.

'Nous in itself knows itself by participating in what it knows; for by touching and knowing it, it comes to be known itself, so that Nous and what it knows are the same thing. For what is receptive of what is known and of Being-ness is Nous. And in possessing [them both] it is all energy, activity, and actuality (*energei*)' – and 'what perfects this energy, activity, and actuality is pleasure'[138] – 'And so it will be this [energy, activity, and actuality, which is Joy] rather than that [Nous and the Being-ness it knows] that seems to be that [truly] divine [state of being] which Nous possesses. And it is the contemplation [of this] that is superlatively pleasurable and supremely good. If, then, it is thus that God possesses the Good in eternity, even as we do on occasion, it is wonderful indeed: if even more so, it is yet more marvellous. But this is just how it is. And [in him] there is life too: for the actuality, activity, and energy of Nous is life; and [God][139] is himself that energy and actuality. Actuality and energy in themselves are indeed God's supremely good and eternal life. And so we roundly affirm that God is a living being, eternal and supremely good, and that in God there is life and coherent, eternal Being. For that is God.'[140]

This is the 'God of the philosophers and scientists' whom Pascal spurned. Or rather it is the God of *the* Philosopher, the rational God of a divine man whose heritage we are doing our best to forget either in a mad rush in pursuit of Dionysian frenzy or in a pseudo-rationalism which prefers to ignore that element of pure chance which disturbed Aristotle so much, threw modern physics into disarray, and which Einstein refused to face. This refusal to adjust theory to newly discovered facts by a man as divine as Aristotle, or nearly so, might have seemed to that marvellously cautious thinker as *atopon pös* – 'in some sense strange, incongruous, absurd'.

Aristotle claimed to have known God 'for a short time' only, but that was enough. He was never so immodest as to claim that he had known the 'Truth', for he knew that this is reserved for God alone.

Chapter 8

The Holy and Undivided Trinity

BEING A SERMON DELIVERED ON TRINITY SUNDAY
1974 AT CORPUS CHRISTI COLLEGE, OXFORD

People of the Book, do not exceed all bounds in your religion
and do not say anything about God except the truth. The
Messiah, son of Mary, is only a Messenger of God and his
Word that he committed to Mary and a Spirit from him. So
believe in God and his Messengers: and do not say: 'Three'.
Refrain: that will be better for you. God is one God only,
glory to him: far be it from him to have a son.

Perhaps this is the first time that a preacher in your chapel has
selected as his theme a text from the sacred book of a non-Christian
religion, in this case the Koran, which the Muslims hold to be
the Word made Book quite as firmly as Christians believe that
Jesus Christ is the Word made man. This paradox I will not
discuss today, for it would take us too far afield. The point of
our text is, however, that in this one verse the Koran refers to
the two specifically Christian doctrines that set Christianity
apart from and in flat opposition to the two strictly monotheistic
religions with which it is related: the Incarnation and the Holy
Trinity whose feast we celebrate today. Both are a stumbling-
block to the Jews and sheer stupidity to the Greeks, as St Paul
was the first to realise. For the Muslims matters were not quite
so simple. That Jesus was the last and the greatest of the prophets
before Muhammad they gladly accepted. Indeed, as our text
shows, they went much further: he is 'God's Word that he
committed to Mary and a Spirit from him', a formula that would
have satisfied Tertullian at least, who made no clear distinction
between the Word and the Spirit. However, it is not with the

Koranic view of the nature of Jesus that we are concerned but with its flat rejection of the doctrine of the Trinity. 'Do not exceed all bounds in your religion . . . and do not say: "Three". Refrain: that would be better for you.' Indeed it would. So why do we not refrain but insist on clinging to this doctrine which we admit we do not understand, which is contrary to reason, and for which there appears to be precious little authority in the New Testament? *making 'Brahman'*

Even if it were true that there are three Persons in one God (and I have never understood how the Holy Spirit – the Holy *Breath*, that is – can conceivably be a 'Person' in any sense of that word) what possible difference can it make to you and me? And if it does in fact make no difference, why should we, in these hyper-ecumenical days, insist on a doctrine which we cannot explain and which is so offensive to the unqualified monotheism of our kindred religions, Judaism and Islam? We admit that the whole thing is a mystery, so why has the Church taken such pains to define the mystery with a more than pedantic precision, each new definition being more preposterous than the last? Personally I simply do not know, but I do believe in the Trinity *pos,* 'in some sense' as Aristotle would say.

Nowadays it is not enough to say with Tertullian: 'It must needs be believed because it is absurd' and that 'it is certain because it is impossible.' You might as well say with the White Queen in *Alice through the Looking-Glass*: 'Sometimes I've believed as many as six impossible things before breakfast.' She was, however, sensible enough not to say that she believed impossible things *because* they were impossible: you have apparently to be a father of the Church to say that. Nevertheless, that, apparently, is precisely what we do and the more we define the mystery, the more absurd does it appear.

As a pre-Conciliar Roman Catholic I never had any difficulty in believing any number of impossible things before or after breakfast. Things, unfortunately, are rather different now, since what was once described as the Roman obedience now looks very much more like the Roman disobedience, and Roman Catholics are at last permitted, if not encouraged, to think for themselves. I am not sure that they do it very well.

However, to return to the particular impossibility that concerns us. 'The Father is incomprehensible, the Son is incomprehensible, the Holy Spirit is incomprehensible: and yet not three incomprehensibles but one Incomprehensible.' In the matter of incomprehensibility I agree as I do in the matter of the Holy Spirit. But the Father and the Son?

The Father and the Son are, of course, essentially Christian terms: the whole of popular Christianity revolves round this relationship. Except among the Quakers and Pentecostalists the Holy Spirit appears rather as an afterthought, perhaps because there is nothing particularly Christian about him. He is specifically named and recognised in the Koran, and as the life-giving afflatus that animates and inspires (breathes into) the universe he is recognised in one form or another in all religions. The 'Father' too is a term metaphorically used of the sky-god in most religions, the god who fertilises Mother Earth: but this is a metaphor.

One thing that is indisputably true about a 'father' is, of course, that he is male; and even a Muslim who abhors the use of the terms 'Father' and 'Son' as in any way applicable to God concedes that in the case of the Virgin Mary God must have provided the equivalent of the male element which alone makes conception possible. Even so they would never use the word 'begat' of this essentially miraculous operation since to 'beget' is not possible without copulation, and, for the Muslim, this is both blasphemous and impossible as applied to God. Hence, if it is blasphemous to speak of God as 'begetter', it is equally blasphemous to speak of 'the Messiah, Son of Mary', as being 'begotten'. Jesus is the 'son' of no one except Mary in that his physical being derives wholly from her: there was no begetting in the ordinary sense. Hence, the Muslims think it is misleading in the case of the man Jesus to speak of his relationship to God as being that of Son to Father, for this implies physical sexual intercourse. This is why the Koran, in affirming the absolute unity of God roundly declares: 'Say, He is God, One, God, the Eternal: he has never begotten nor has he ever been begotten, and like unto him is there none, – no, not one.'[2]

This short chapter of the Koran is probably directed much more against the idea of Christ as the second Person of the Trinity than against the man Jesus, son of Mary, since the idea of 'begetting' and being 'begotten' within the Godhead itself seemed to the Muslims both blasphemous and absurd. In all this I find myself in agreement with the Muslims: to speak of the

140   *The City Within the Heart*

Trinity as Father, Son, and Holy Spirit seems to me misleading
to a degree that is quite unacceptable to any rational animal.

Is it any better if we substitute the Johannine 'Word' for
'Son'? Not much, so long as we continue to use the English
word 'Word' to translate the Greek *Logos*. The amount of
confusion that the impossible idea of the 'Word made Flesh' has
caused among Christians (let alone among non-Christians)
scarcely bears thinking of. Of all the possible translations of
Logos, 'Word' would seem to be far the worst, and that the
perpetrators of the New English Bible should have chosen to
keep it seems about as incomprehensible as the Holy Trinity
itself.

The Johannine *Logos* must of course reflect the Stoic *Logos*
which the Stoics themselves derived from Heraclitus and for
both it meant something like 'the true account of the law of the
universe' or as the Epistle to the Colossians puts it 'he [who]
holds all things in unity', or again 'the perfect copy of [God's]
nature, sustaining the universe by his powerful command', as the
Epistle to the Hebrews has it. *Mutatis mutandis* this is the *Nous*
of Anaxagoras and ever more so the $\dfrac{\pi\acute{o}\bar{\epsilon}\sigma\iota\varsigma}{\nu\acute{o}\eta\delta\iota\varsigma}$ $\dfrac{\pi\acute{o}\bar{\epsilon}\varsigma\epsilon\bar{o}\varsigma}{\nu o\acute{\eta}\delta\epsilon\omega\varsigma}$ of
Aristotle to which we will return. The Father and the Son,
then, to which the literal-minded Muslims so strongly objected,
can be seen as a symbol for 'the true account of the law of the
universe', the principle of rationality that operates throughout
the universe (the 'Son') and that even higher principle which
projects this 'mind' into the universe (the 'Father'). Call them
'Father' and 'Son' if you like, but if you do so you should not
be surprised if non-Christians think you are crazy.

So much for the Father and the Son. What of the Holy Spirit?

As I have said the Holy Spirit presents few problems so far as
the non-Christian religions are concerned. But what is its position
within the Trinity itself? Here again I think some light can be
thrown on it by reference to another non-Christian religion, this
time Hinduism.

Now the dominant philosophy within Hinduism is known as
Vedānta, and in its most currently accepted form this is a
philosophy of pure monism, the tenets of which correspond
almost exactly to the basic insight of our own Parmenides,
namely that there is only one Reality – One without a second –

apart from which all else is, from the absolute point of view, simply non-existent. This is pure monism, not even monotheism, since God himself, in this frame of reference, is non-existent, or, more precisely, the non-existent Lord of a non-existent universe. What, then, are you and I? Insofar as we think we are you and I, we are simply non-existent, *but* insofar as we exist at all, we *are* the One without a second. Thus we are identically One and there is no difference at all: or in the celebrated words of the *Chāndogya* Upanishad: 'That you are.' Or, to put these lapidary words into their proper context:

'All these creatures [here] have Being as their root, Being as their resting-place, Being as their foundation . . .

'This finest essence – the whole universe has as its Self: That is the Real: That is the Self: That *you* are.'

In other words, in your essence, you are the One without a second, pure Being without any trace of becoming, for that is the only Reality: or in yet other words the ground of your being is *identical* with the ground of the Godhead: it is One, and it is pure Being without a trace of becoming. And this too seems to be absurd.

The monism of the Vedanta is often compared with the apophatic theology of Pseudo-Dionysius, who had such an immense influence on medieval theology and mysticism, and the comparison does indeed hold good. But the Vedanta, despite the fact that it says that ultimately the Absolute is utterly beyond words, is, like all mysticism and all philosophy, compelled to use words as pointers to the ineffable reality; and the formula it reached, which was accepted by all schools of the Vedanta, was *Sat-Cit-Ānanda*, Being – Thought – Joy, an *im*personal Trinity inhering in and absolutely inseparable from the absolute One.

Sat, 'Being': this presents little difficulty. In the sacred texts, unlike the rigid monism of a later school, this means the Unmoved One from which all becoming, all movement proceeds – the Unmoved Mover of Aristotle. By analogy you are perfectly entitled to call it the 'Father' (but not, please, in the company of Muslims), since Aristotle himself did not find the term inappropriate.

Next *Cit*, 'Thought': God's thinking of himself, God's consciousness of himself, God's awareness of himself (for *cit* can mean all these); in other words God's *Logos*, the 'true account

Consciousness

of [God's] universe', in which, through which, and for which (cf. Col. 1.16) the universe exists. This again is Aristotle's $\dfrac{\pi o\bar{\varepsilon}\varsigma\iota\varsigma}{\nu o\eta\delta\iota\varsigma}\ \dfrac{\pi o\bar{\varepsilon}\varsigma\varepsilon\bar{o}\varsigma}{\nu o\eta\delta\varepsilon\omega\varsigma}$, God's thinking of his own thinking and of himself, his awareness of himself and of what he thinks: and what he thinks is the rational order of the universe, that is, the *Logos*.

And now *Ānanda*, 'Joy', which in one of the Upanishads[3] is the highest manifestation of the Godhead, higher even than 'understanding', higher than *Logos*, higher even than Aristotle's *Nous*; for 'once a man has tasted this savour, he tastes joy. For who could breathe, who could live, were this joy not [diffused] throughout space?' But the Sanskrit word *ānanda* means not only 'joy' but also the specific joy a man enjoys in the embrace of his wife, precisely and exactly what the Christian mystics mean by the joy the human soul experiences when its spiritual marriage with God is consummated. This Joy, then, is also passionate love, the yearning that is yet always fulfilled within the Godhead itself, what Aristotle does not shrink from calling *hēdonē*, 'pleasure', the supreme pleasure that God enjoys in eternity through his self-realisation in his *Nous*, that is, his *Logos*. This pleasure, this indwelling joy, is that God who, according to St John, *is* Love: it is the Holy Spirit which is the bond of union that unites and *identifies* the divine Thinker with his *Logos* so that now there is no duality but only one single Godhead in whom Being, Awareness, and the Joy of Love are one and the same thing; and this is what Aristotle calls God's *energeia*, his 'actuality', activity, and the effortless energy with which he contemplates himself. So let us leave the last word on the subject of the Most Holy and Undivided Trinity to Aristotle himself, the father of our rational civilisation and stepfather of the Catholic Church.

'And so', he says, 'it will be this [energy, activity, and actuality which is joy] rather than that Nous, [that awareness and understanding of Being and of all things], which seems to be that [truly] divine thing which *Nous* possesses. Hence it is contemplation that is supremely joyous and supremely good. If, then, it is thus that God possesses the good in eternity, even as we can do so on occasion, it is wonderful indeed: if even more so, then it is yet more marvellous. But this is just how it is. And [in him] there is life too: for the actuality, activity, and energy of this *Nous* is life, and it is itself that very actuality, activity, and energy. . . . And so we roundly affirm that God is a living being, eternal and supremely good, and that in God there is life and coherent eternal being. For that *is* God.'[4] Being, Awareness, Joy-in-Love: Three in One, and One in Three: your God and my God, the God of the Hindus and the God of Aristotle.

Being - constancy
higher mind /
Empathy empathy - bliss

Notes

Chapter 1   Which God Is Dead?

1   C. G. Jung, *Memories, Dreams, and Reflections*, Collins and Routledge & Kegan Paul, 1963, p. 64.
2   S.C.M. Press, 1973.
3   Quoted by William James, *The Varieties of Religious Experience*, 1902, and reprints Lecture xvi.
4   Aristotle, *Metaphysics*, xii (1072b).
5   *Udāna*, pp. 80–81.
6   *Mundaka Upanishad*, 1, 2, 8.
7   *Chandogya Upanishad*, 8, 14.
8   *ibid.*, 6, 8, 7 *ff*.
9   William James, *op. cit.*, Lecture xvi.
10   *Brihadāranyaka Upanishad*, 1, 3, 28.
11   Lamentations, 3, 38.

Chapter 2   Mysticism without Love

1   See my *Hindu and Muslim Mysticism*, Athlone Press, London, p. 135.
2   Aristotle, *Metaphysics*, 1051 a18.
3   Very common in Pāli Canon, esp. *Samyutta Nikāya* iii and iv.
4   *Brihadāranyaka Upanishad*, 2, 1, 20.
5   R. C. Zaehner, *Mysticism Sacred and Profane*, Clarendon Press, 1957.
6   Aristotle, *Nicomachean Ethics*, 1178 b20.
7   *Chādogya Upanishad*, 8, 11, 2.
8   Plato, *Phaedo*, 64 A.
9   *Mandūkya Upanishad*, 7.
10   Aristotle, *Metaphysics*, 1074 b35.
11   *Śvetāśvatara Upanishad*, 5, 1.

Chapter 3   The Wickedness of Evil

1   D. Bonhoeffer, *Letters and Papers from Prison*, S.C.M. Press, 1953.
2   Pierre Teilhard de Chardin, *Letters To Two Friends, 1926–1954*, Collins, 1972, p. 146.
3   D. Bonhoeffer, *op. cit.*, p. 157.
4   C. G. Jung, *Answer To Job*, Routledge & Kegan Paul, 1954, pp. 3–4; Collected Works, Vol. xi.
5   *Joshua*, 6. 21.
6   *1 Samuel*, 15. 3.
7   *Job*, 39.
8   *Isaiah*, 45. 7.

9   C. G. Jung, *op. cit.*, p. 10.
10 *Isaiah*, 55. 8–9.
11 *Udāna*, p. 81.
12 R. M. Bucke, *Cosmic Consciousness*, 23rd. ed., E. P. Dutton, New York, p. 17.
13 George Bernanos, *Sous le Soleil De Satan*. p. 154.
14 Hui Nêng, *The Platform Scripture*, Tr. Wing-Tsit Chan, St. John's University Press, New York, 1963, p. 147.
15 J. Kennett, *Selling Water by the River*, Allen & Unwin, 1973, p. 56.
16 Quoted in Guinness, *The Dust of Death*, Inter-Varsity Press, 1973, p. 192.
17 *Tai Hiriya*, p. 2. 1.
18 *Kanshitaki*, p. 3. 1.
19 *Bhagavad Gitā*, 18. 17.
20 For this and other references to Charles Manson and his friends, I have used contemporary newspaper reports and Ed Sanders, *The Family*, Rupert Hart Davis, 1972 and George Bishop, *Witness to Evil*, Nash Publishing, Los Angeles, 1971.
21 Philip Kapleau, *The Three Pillars of Zen*, Harper and Row, New York, 1966, p. 206.
22 *Brihadāranyaka Upanishad*, 4.4.19.
23 Arthur Waley, *The Way and Its Power*, Allen & Unwin, 1934, p. 167.
24 P. E. L. Masters and Jean Houston, *The Varieties of Psychedelic Experience*, Anthony Blond, 1966, p. 243.
25 *Brihadāranyaka Upanishad*, 1.4.10.
26 *ibid.*, 2.4.15.
27 Aristotle, *Metaphysics*, 075 a12–15.
28 *Revelation*, 19. 13–15.
29 A free rendering of Prof. Charlotte Vandeville's translation *Kabir* published by the Clarendon Press.

Chapter 4   Tantum religio potuit suadere malorum

1   Al-Sulami, ed. N. Sudayba, Cairo, 1953, pp. 72–73.
2   Lucretius, *De Rerum Natura*, 1. 62–78.
3   *Genesis*, 3. 5.
4   Lucretius, *op. cit.*, 1. 82–83.
5   Plato, *Phaedo*, 70 A.
6   *Brihadāranyaka Upanishad*, 2.4.12.
7   *Ecclesiastes*, 8. 15 (NEB).
8   *ibid.*, 9. 10.
9   Lucretius, *op. cit.*, 1. 102–111.
10 *Isaiah*, 45. 7.
11 *Joshua*, 6. 17, 21.
12 *1 Samuel*, 15. 1–35.
13 *ibid.*, 15. 35 (NEB).
14 *ibid.*, 18. 10.
15 *Matthew*, 10. 34–35.
16 *Koran*, 7. 177.

17   *ibid.*, 32. 13.
18   *ibid.*, 50. 29.

Chapter 5   *The Scandal of Christ*

1   *1 Corinthians*, 1. 23
2   Euripides, *Electra*, 1035.
3   *Deuteronomy*, 5. 6, etc.
4   *cf.* 1. *Samuel*, 10. 10, the 'company of prophets' who inspired Saul to 'prophetic rapture' (NEB).
5   *Jerusalem Bible*, p. 1117.
6   *Ecclesiastes*, 9. 5.
7   See especially Psalm 88.
8   *Koran*, 3. 43; 5. 109.
9   *ibid.*, 4. 156, which, however, does not agree with 3. 48 where it is said that God causes Jesus to die and then raises him up to himself.
10   *ibid.*, 2. 107.
11   *ibid.*, 19. 35.
12   *ibid.*, 4. 169.
13   *ibid.*, 3. 184; 5. 16.
14   *Aitareya Upanishad*, 5. 3.
15   *De Incarnatione*, 54.
16   *Digha Nikaya*, 221–222. Mrs T. W. Rhys Davids, *Dialogues of the Buddha*, O.U.P. pp. 281–282.

Chapter 6   *Why not Islam?*

1   Aristotle, *Politics*, 1297 a11.
2   Wilfrid Cantwell Smith, *Questions of Religious Truth*, Charles Scribner & Sons, New York, 1967, pp. 39–62.
·3   *ibid.*, p. 56.
4   *ibid.*, pp. 40–41.
5   A. J. Arberry, *The Doctrine of the Sūfis*, Cambridge, 1935.
6   *Koran*, 12. 1; 28. 1; 43. 1; 44. 1, etc.
7   *ibid.*, 12. 2; 43. 2; 13. 37, etc.
8   *ibid.*, 3. 5.
9   Al-Kalābādhi, *Al-ta'arruf li-madhhab ahl al-tasawwuf*, ed. A. Mahmud and T. A. Surud, Cairo, 1960, p. 39. *cf* A. J. Arberry, *op. cit.* p. 21.
10   *ibid.*, text, p. 41: tr. p. 23.
11   *Koran*, 2. 70; 9. 6; 48. 15.
12   Al-Kalābādhi, text, pp. 40–41; trs. pp. 22–23.
13   *Koran*, 3. 52.
14   *ibid.*, 3. 40–2.
15   *ibid.*, 2. 32.
16   *ibid.*, 3. 40; 4. 169.
17   *ibid.*, 4. 169.
18   *ibid.*
19   E. Hussey, *The Presocratics*, Duckworth, 1972, p. 40.

20 *Koran*, 4. 169.
21 See note 2 above.
22 *Koran*, 5. 116.
23 *ibid.*, 20. 120.
24 *Koran*, 33. 28–52.
25 *Acts*, 5. 39 (NEB).

Chapter 7   The God of the Philosopher

1   Quoted in Freud's *Civilisation and its Discontents*: Standard Edition, vol. xxi, pp. 64–65.
2   *Brihadāranyaka Upanishad*, 4.3.32.
3   Fragment 11, cited by Edward Hussey, *The Presocratics*, Duckworth, 1972, p. 13.
4   *ibid.*
5   *ibid.*
6   *Genesis*, 6. 2. The New English Bible prefers 'sons of the gods'.
7   See above.
8   *Tao Tê Ching*, 16. 52 tr. Arthur Waley, *The Way and its Power*, Allen & Unwin, 1934.
9   *cf.* W. B. Henning, *Transactions of the Philological Society*, 1945, pp. 108–18.
10 *Brihadāranyaka Upanishad*, 1.5.22: 'Just as breath holds the midmost position between the human faculties, so does the wind among natural phenomena: for the other natural phenomena fade away; not so the wind.'
11 *op. cit.*, 2.3.6.
12 *Colossians*, 1. 15.
13 *Ecclesiastes*, 9. 5.
14 *Odyssey*, 11. 488–9.
15 *Atharva Veda*, 18.3.3. For further information see A. A. Macdonell, *Vedic Mythology*, Strassburg, 1897, p. 169.
16 *Ecclesiastes*, 8. 15.
17 *op. cit.*, 12. 13.
18 *Brihadāranyaka Upanishad*, 4.3.14.
19 On this whole subject see E. R. Dodds, *The Greeks and the Irrational*, Chapter V.
20 *I Samuel*, 10. 10.
21 R. C. Zaehner, *Our Savage God*, Collins, 1974, Chapter IV.
22 (Pseudo-) Aristotle, *On the Cosmos*, 396. 620.
23 K. Marx and F. Engels, *On Religion*, Moscow, 1957, p. 38.
24 Aristotle, *Nicomachean Ethics*, 1146 b30.
25 Fragment 93, E. Hussey, *op. cit.*, p. 37.
26 *ibid.*, Fr. 50; tr. p. 39.
27 *John*, 17. 21.
28 Heraclitus, Fr. 1: Hussey, p. 39.
29 *Brihadāranyaka Upanishad*, 4.3.20.
30 Heraclitus, Fr. 10; Hussey, *op. cit.*, p. 45.
31 Heraclitus, Fr. 80; Hussey, *op. cit.*, p. 48.

32   Aristotle, *Physics*, 185 b20–5.

33   *ibid.*, 186 a 1–3.

34   *Brihadāranyaka Upanishad*, 4.4.19–20: *cf. Katha Upanishad*, 4. 10–11.

35   Parmenides, Fr. 1; E. Hussey, *op. cit.*, p. 79.

36   *Brihadāranyaka Upanishad*, 3.8.11.

37   Parmenides, Fr. 2, 6; E. Hussey, *op. cit.*, pp. 81, 83. I have slightly modified Hussey's translation in places.

38   *Katha Upanishad*, 6. 12.

39   Parmenides, Fr. 8; E. Hussey, *op. cit.*, p. 88.

40   Parmenides, Fr. 6; E. Hussey, *op. cit.*, p. 86.

41   Nagarjuna, *Madhyamaka-karikas*, 24. 8–9. Text and translation in Kenneth K. Inada, *Nagarajuna*, Tokyo, 1970, p. 146.

42   See E. Hussey, *op. cit.*, p. 128.

43   Aristotle, *On the Heavens*, 270 b6.

44   *ibid., op. cit.*, 271 a34.

45   *op. cit.*, 270 b15.

46   Aristotle, *Physics*, 199 a33–199 b5.

47   *ibid., Rhetoric*, 1391 b2.

48   *ibid., Nicomachean Ethics*, 1099 b11.

49   *ibid.*, 1179 a24.

50   *ibid., Metaphysics*, 1074 b1–14.

51   *ibid., Politics*, 1328 b12.

52   *ibid.*, 1329 a29–34.

53   *ibid., Nicomachean Ethics*, 1153 b32.

54   *ibid., Generation of Animals*, 761 a5.

55   *ibid., Parts of Animals*, 656 a8.

56   *ibid., Nicomachean Ethics*, 1162 a17.

57   *ibid., Metaphysics*, 1032 a22.

58   *ibid., Physics*, 192 a3–6.

59   *ibid., On Coming to be and Passing away*, 318 b16.

60   I previously translated this difficult passage in *Our Savage God* (Collins, 1974) p. 168. The translation, I now feel convinced, was wrong. As Aristotle has explained in the two preceding paragraphs, there are two senses to the words *to mē on*, 'what is not': it is either 'matter' or *sterēsis*. What desires 'form' must be matter, since absolute *sterēsis*, being absolute nothingness, is opposed (*enantion*) to the 'divine, good, and desirable' in the text. *Enantion* is not, I now think, used in the sense of 'contrariety', but of what is wholly opposed to the divine. The second *enantion* must, however, mean 'one of the pairs of opposites', since these 'are mutually destructive'. It cannot here mean *sterēsis*, for what negates God cannot destroy him since he is undestructible. It can only negate and destroy its opposite as cold negates and destroys hot.

61   Aristotle, *Generation of Animals*, 737 a27.

62   *ibid.*, Physics, 192 a13.

63   *ibid., Generation of Animals*, 716 a7, 729 a11 and *passim*.

64   *ibid., On the Soul*, 414 a13.

65   *ibid.*, 414 a20: *cf.* 412 a4 *ff.*

66   *ibid.*, 413 b25.

67   *ibid.*, 412 b11–17.

68 *ibid., Generation of Animals,* 736 b28.
69 *ibid., On the Heavens,* 270 b23.
70 *ibid., Generation of Animals,* 736 a19–21.
71 *ibid., Rhetoric,* 1390 b11.
72 *ibid., Eudemian Ethics,* 1249 b17.
73 *ibid., Nicomachean Ethics,* 1104 b31.
74 *ibid.,* 1100 b29–32.
75 *ibid., Rhetoric,* 1389 a.
76 See above. (75)
77 For the use of *theōria* and *theatrikos* in this sense see *Politics,* 1342 a17–22.
78 See above. (77)
79 *Luke,* 10. 42.
80 Aristotle, *Politics,* 13333 a36.
81 *ibid.,* 1177 b4.
82 *ibid., Generation of Animals,* 760 b30–3.
83 *ibid., On the Soul,* 431 b21.
84 See below. (85)
85 Aristotle, *On the Soul,* 432 a1.
86 *Brihadāranyaka Upanishad,* 4.5.15.
87 *ibid.,* 1.4.10.
88 'Pure' is not in the Greek. 'Actuality', 'activity', and 'energy' are all implied in the single Greek word *energeia.*
89 Aristotle, *On the Soul,* 430 a10–25.
90 *ibid., Eudemian Ethics,* 1248 a25–8.
91 *ibid., Metaphysics,* 1075 a15.
92 *ibid., op. cit.,* 1072 a29; 1072 b4.
93 *ibid., op. cit.,* 1072 a26–30.
94 *ibid., On the Soul,* 432 a2.
95 Sermon 2.
96 Aristotle, *Eudemian Ethics,* 1249 b17.
97 *ibid., op. cit.,* 1242 a34.
98 *ibid., Metaphysics,* 1075 a12–17.
99 *ibid., Eudemian Ethics,* 1238 b28–32.
100 *ibid., Nicomachean Ethics,* 1167 b18.
101 *ibid., op. cit.,* 1167 b32.
102 *ibid., op. cit.,* 1167 b34–1168 a10.
103 *ibid., Metaphysics,* 1074 a36.
104 *ibid., op. cit.,* 1074 b35.
105 *ibid., Nicomachean Ethics,* 1170 b6.
106 *ibid., Politics,* 1334 b20 etc.
107 *ibid., Nicomachean Ethics,* 1139 a19.
108 *ibid., Eudemian Ethics,* 1240 b37.
109 *ibid., Nicomachean Ethics,* 1166 a14.
110 *ibid., op. cit.,* 1166 a31.
111 *ibid., Eudemian Ethics,* 1246 b36.
112 *ibid., op. cit.,* 1248 a38.
113 *ibid., op. cit.,* 1247 b35.
114 *ibid., op. cit.,* 1235 b32.
115 *ibid., Nicomachean Ethics,* 1169 b18.

116   *ibid., op. cit.,* 1166 a18–23.
117   *ibid., op. cit.,* 1153 a1.
118   *ibid., op. cit.,* 1170 b29.
119   *ibid., op. cit.,* 1171 a5.
120   *ibid., op. cit.,* 1171 a12.
121   *ibid., Eudemian Ethics,* 1249 b14–21.
122   *ibid., op. cit.,* 1249 b21–4.
123   *ibid., op. cit.,* 1246 b36.
124   *ibid., op. cit.,* 1248 a29.
125   *ibid., op. cit.,* 1247 a28–9.
126   *ibid., op. cit.,* 1248 a31–4.
127   Or 'what is'.
128   Aristotle, *Eudemian Ethics,* 1248 a38–b7.
129   *ibid., Poetics,* 1449 b27.
130   *ibid., Politics,* 1342 a4–15.
131   *ibid., Poetics,* 1455 a35.
132   *Sāmkhya-kārikā,* 66.
133   *ibid.,* 59–62.
134   The three words translate the Greek *energeia.*
135   Aristotle, *Metaphysics,* 1072 b14–17.
136   *ibid., Eudemian Ethics,* 139 a30–41.
137   See above. (136)
138   Aristotle, *Nicomachean Ethics,* 1174 b23–4.
139   I now take *ekeinos* to refer to God rather than Nous since *theos* is the penultimate masculine noun in the text.
140   Aristotle, *Metaphysics,* 1072 b20–31.

Chapter 8   *The Holy and Undivided Trinity*

1   *Koran,* 4. 169.
2   *ibid.,* 112.
3   Taittiriya Upanishad, 2. 5–7.
4   Aristotle, Metaphysics, 1072 b.

Index